SYMBOL, MYTH, AND RITUAL

Series Editor: Victor Turner

KARAVAR

Masks and Power in
a Melanesian Ritual

SYMBOL, MYTH, AND RITUAL SERIES

Frederick Karl Errington, *Karavar: Masks and Power in a Melanesian Ritual*

Shlomo Deshen and Moshe Shokeid, *The Predicament of Homecoming: Cultural and Social Life of North African Immigrants in Israel*

Barbara G. Myerhoff, *Peyote Hunt: The Sacred Journey of the Huichol Indians*

Victor Turner, *Dramas, Fields, and Metaphors: Symbolic Action in Human Society*

Frank E. Manning, *Black Clubs in Bermuda: Ethnography of a Play World*

Raymond Firth, *Symbols: Public and Private*

Nancy D. Munn, *Walbiri Iconography: Graphic Representation and Cultural Symbolism in a Central Australian Society*

Mircea Eliade, *Australian Religions: An Introduction*

KARAVAR

Masks and Power in a
Melanesian Ritual

Frederick Karl Errington

Cornell University Press
ITHACA AND LONDON

First published 1974 by Cornell University Press.
Published in the United Kingdom by Cornell University Press Ltd.,
2-4 Brook Street, London W1Y 1AA.

International Standard Book Number 0-8014-0836-9
Library of Congress Catalog Card Number 74-3997

Printed in the United States of America by Vail-Ballou Press, Inc.

TO SHELLY

Foreword

Recently both the research and theoretical concerns of many anthropologists have once again been directed toward the role of symbols—religious, mythic, aesthetic, political, and even economic—in social and cultural processes. Whether this revival is a belated response to developments in other disciplines (psychology, ethology, philosophy, linguistics, to name only a few), or whether it reflects a return to a central concern after a period of neglect, is difficult to say. In recent field studies, anthropologists have been collecting myths and rituals in the context of social action, and improvements in anthropological field technique have produced data that are richer and more refined than heretofore; these new data have probably challenged theoreticians to provide more adequate explanatory frames. Whatever may have been the causes, there is no denying a renewed curiosity about the nature of the connections between culture, cognition, and perception, as these connections are revealed in symbolic forms.

Although excellent individual monographs and articles in symbolic anthropology or comparative symbology have recently appeared, a common focus or forum that can be provided by a topically organized series of books has not been available. The present series is intended to fill this lacuna. It is designed to include not only field monographs and theoretical and comparative studies by anthropologists, but also work by scholars in other disciplines, both scientific and humanistic. The appearance of studies in such a forum encourages emulation, and emulation can produce fruitful new theories. It is therefore our hope that the series will serve as a house of many mansions, providing hospitality for the practitioners of any discipline that has a serious and creative concern with comparative symbology. Too often, disciplines are sealed off, in sterile pedantry, from significant intellectual influences. Nevertheless, our primary aim is to bring to public attention works on ritual and myth written by anthropologists, and our readers will find a variety of strictly anthropological approaches ranging from formal analyses of systems of symbols to empathetic accounts of divinatory and initiatory rituals.

Frederick Errington argues forcefully, in this study of the mortuary rituals of the Melanesian Karavar people of the Bismarck Archipelago, that in the absence of an indigenous concept of social structure "meaning comes through social activity: epistemological problems are practical problems." Specifically, for Karavarans, nonritual life is concerned with exercising power while ritual is concerned with constraining it. Karavaran beliefs emerge in action; cosmology is rudimentarily developed; *parole* dominates *langue;* operation subdues exegesis. This culture is essentially "performative." It *works* with its words, it is nonreflexive, and it has "no abstract political theory." Ritual is not "a statement of order" but an "ordering." Ritual symbols achieve efficacy through their use at a specific time and in a given place, and their meaning is "inherent in and not apart from activity."

To understand Karavaran culture, Errington says, we must grasp it integrally through its own basic terms, *momboto* ("antisociety"), *divara* ("shell money," an image and instrument of "ordering" used mainly in ritual exchange), *duk-duk* ("male ritual figure"), *tubuan* ("female ritual figure"), and so on, as these terms are translated into action in different kinds of social situations. If we make this effort we will find that for the Karavarans order is always problematic, never to be assumed, and has continually to be re-created in the teeth of anarchic *momboto* forces. Ritual action is, perhaps, the most potent ordering instrument, and its symbols have meaning mainly in the actual ordering process. Errington's presentation of the Karavaran view, which does not see social order as resting on structure, "either social structure or personal character structure," is a healthy corrective to the anthropological perspective which assumes that social order does have such origins and that ritual symbols derive their meanings from some abstract cosmological schema. The wheel has come full circle with Errington; we are back to R. R. Marett's view that "the rite is danced out, not thought out," but with one crucial difference. For Errington, the rite is danced out not in response to mute archaic instincts but with and for order and power in the pragmatic here and now.

VICTOR TURNER

University of Chicago

Contents

Preface 13
Introduction 19

PART ONE | THE CONCEPT AND EXERCISE OF
 POWER

 1. Kinship 35
 2. Male-Female Relations 58
 3. The Vurkurai Court 66

PART TWO | THE RITUAL FOUNDATIONS OF THE
 CONCEPT AND EXERCISE OF POWER

 4. Ritual Grades 79
 5. Preliminary Stages in the Mortuary Cycle 122
 6. Initial Stages in the Utuan Matamatam 141
 7. Construction of the Tubuan and Dukduk 166
 8. Big Men and the Tubuan 206
 9. Conclusion 243

Glossary 251
Appendix: Calendar of Events at the Utuan Matamatam 254
Bibliography 255
Index 257

Illustrations

MAP

Duke of York Islands   20

PLATES

1. Ambo speaking at nangwan   147
2. Ambo, Doti, Otia, Tomiton, and Alipet—some of the
   Karavaran and Utuan big men   149
3. Thatched ceremonial house at taraiu   179
4. Distribution of divara to women for cooking   184
5. Tubuan and canoes offshore on the kinivai   214
6. Karavarans landing on Utuan at conclusion of the
   kinivai   215
7. Doti's butur, dancing ground, and slit gong   220
8. Tubuan in the village   221
9. Greeting a dukduk with lime powder in the village   222
10. Tubuans and dukduks kneeling for the tutupur   226
11. Tutupur   227
12. Tubuans dancing to male chorus   237

FIGURES

1. Kinship terms   36
2. Twembe and Ialu's genealogy   47
3. Alipet's genealogy   54
4. Genealogy of the Doti, Mesak, Koi group   152
5. Genealogy of the Dengit, Alipati group   155
6. Genealogy of the Bangut, Minio, Tande group   158
7. Genealogy of the Mundiaro, Tomtun, Tomitawa
   group   159

Preface

Societies throughout Melanesia are characterized by the activities of "big men" (men of first importance) and their followers, who compete with one another for prestige through the exchange of valuables and food. Social order is often precarious, in part because the pattern of intracommunity and intercommunity alliances on which social order is based changes as the fortunes of big men change. Karavar, the southernmost island in the cluster that composes the Duke of York Islands of Papua New Guinea, is typical of Melanesia in these respects, but it is somewhat unusual in that a big man's power is not seen as resting on a wide range of attributes. A Karavaran big man, unlike other Melanesian big men, does not maintain political power primarily through force of manner, physical vigor, gardening skill, or knowledge of magic or sorcery: this latter attribute in particular is of negligible importance. Rather, his power is based primarily on his possession and astute use of shell money, and he will remain a big man as long as his supply of shell money lasts. As a consequence, he does not face the specter of inevitable, total, and ignominious political collapse, and although political life on Karavar is certainly characterized by competition and changing alliances, it is probably more stable than political life in much of Melanesia. Such a relative stability may be the outcome of an extraordinary preoccupation with the creation of order.

My aim in the pages that follow is to examine the social logic that underlies Karavaran nonritual life and the *dukduk* and *tubuan* ritual, much of which is aimed at maintaining this order. It is my belief that Karavaran social reality cannot be understood in structural terms, and I have tried to provide an alternative perspective by which anthropologists can understand this and other societies.

Karavar is a small island about a mile long, measured by a central path that runs the length of the island, and less than half a mile wide. Inhabited by some 225 people, with a growing population, it is fringed by reefs, and fishing is moderately successful. Most of the island is planted to coconuts, which thrive in a way that vegetable crops do not on the thin soil that overlies the coral base. Except for a few small sweet potato plots and stands of greens adjacent to several of the houses, there are no gardens, although there is adequate space. Most of the gardens are on the Mauke portion of the neighboring island of Ulu, which supplies much of the Karavarans' food. Social and political activity among the Duke of York Islands is possible because the distances between these islands are slight, often less than a mile; canoe travel between them is safe and easy except on the infrequently rough seas. New Ireland and New Britain are the largest islands on either side of the Duke of York Islands, and the town of Rabaul, the administrative and commercial center of this area, is only twenty miles away by sea.

The climate of the region is consistently mild. Trade winds provide a slight seasonal change, but rainfall is always more than sufficient for the existing vegetable crops and for the coconuts. Gardens grow throughout the year without seasonal scarcity.

The only other nearby group who have been studied systematically by anthropologists are the Tolai of New Britain's Gazelle Peninsula. Research on the Tolai is reported in *Capitalism: Primitive and Modern* by T. S. Epstein (1968), in *Matupit* by A. L. Epstein (1969), and in *Vunamami* by R. Salisbury (1970b), as well as in a number of articles by the same authors. These sources provide detailed accounts of the history of European contact in this area and often directly concern the Duke of York Islands.

The Tolai are similar in many ways to the people living on the Duke of York Islands. Both speak similar Austronesian languages, use the same shell money, are organized in matrilineal moieties, and employ the dukduk and tubuan figures in their ritual. These two groups differ significantly, however, in the quantities of shell money they use, in the operation of their kinship system, and in the ownership and meaning of the dukduk and tubuan ritual figures.

Because none of these contemporary authors has written in detail about the dukduk and tubuan ritual system among the Tolai, it is impossible to make a full comparison between the Tolai ritual and the Karavaran–Duke of York ritual analyzed in this book. The best accounts of Tolai dukduk and tubuan ritual are in Salisbury's "Politics and Shell-Money Finance in New Britain" (1966) and "Dukduks, Dualism and Descent Groups: The Place of Parkinson in Ethnological Theory" (1970a).

The major field research in Karavar was done with Shelly Errington, extending from January to December 1968 except for a brief period of library research in Australia. In June and July 1972 I conducted additional field work with Richard C. Sandhaus.

Note on Orthography

I have departed slightly from the orthography used for Tolai in order to help the reader to pronounce the Karavaran language more easily. Except at the beginning of a word, all *b* sounds are preceded by an *m* sound: thus the word written in Tolai as *kubak* is actually pronounced *kumbak*. I have inserted *m*'s before all *b*'s except in the word *tubuan* (pronounced *tumbuan*), as this word is already established in anthropological literature.

All *g* sounds are preceded by an *n* sound. If the *n* is written, the *g* is soft, as in English "sing"; for example, *nangwan* is pronounced *nang-wan*. If the *n* is unwritten, the *g* sound is hard, as in English "go"; for example, *tagan* is pronounced *tang-gan*. This corresponds to Tolai orthography.

To reduce complication I have made Karavaran words plural simply by adding "s" rather than by following the more complex Karavaran procedure of pluralization.

Acknowledgments

I am particularly indebted to Shelly Errington, who shared the field work on which this book is based; her clear and imaginative ideas were extremely helpful to me in formulating and refining my analysis. Her ideas are most apparent in my discussion of the Karavaran courts, a discussion which grew directly out of a jointly authored essay. My mother, Carolyn Errington, unstintingly contributed her editorial skills during the revisions of the manuscript. James Siegel contributed to the development of many of my ideas which eventually found expression in this book.

I am grateful to Alan Babb, Joel Ehrenkranz, Donald Pitkin, Ellen Ryerson, and Richard Sandhaus for their critical reading of the manuscript. I am further indebted to Richard Sandhaus for taking and allowing me to use all of the photographs except Plates 6, 7, and 10, which I took.

The Karavarans were kind, patient, and open with us. I would like to thank Wilson and Tomerau, especially, for their concern that I reach a proper understanding and appreciation of Karavaran life.

Field research during 1968 was supported by a grant (MH 11234) and fellowship from the National Institute of Mental Health of the United States Public Health Service. My field research during 1972 was supported by a Miner D. Crary Fellowship from Amherst College.

FREDERICK KARL ERRINGTON

Amherst, Massachusetts

Introduction

Social order in the Karavaran view is achieved only with great effort. Order is not inherent in human life; its presence cannot be assumed. Much of Karavaran social life, especially ritual, is the effort to create and maintain order and to prevent themselves from slipping back into a state of anarchy. They see their social life as a continual effort to tame themselves and others, to channel their desires and energies into orderly paths. Such a view of society rests on their beliefs about the nature of man and the nature of order.

If, as Taylor (1971) and Geertz (1973) argue, beliefs of a people about their own society do not reflect but rather constitute their social reality, the only way to understand their social reality is to understand their beliefs about it. The Karavarans' beliefs about the nature of man and social order reveal their view of what makes society possible at all. These beliefs do not represent a conscious effort to theorize about the nature of society. Because their understanding of their reality has never been in doubt to them, their beliefs about it remain implicit rather than explicit (Geertz 1964:63–64).

The Karavaran view of reality is most clearly incorporated in their view of what we would call time and history. Karavarans believe that "those who went first" (*tara ni munga*) lived in a state called the *momboto*. The momboto is an image of an antisociety. Literally, the term means failure to see clearly: the men living in the momboto could not see the path

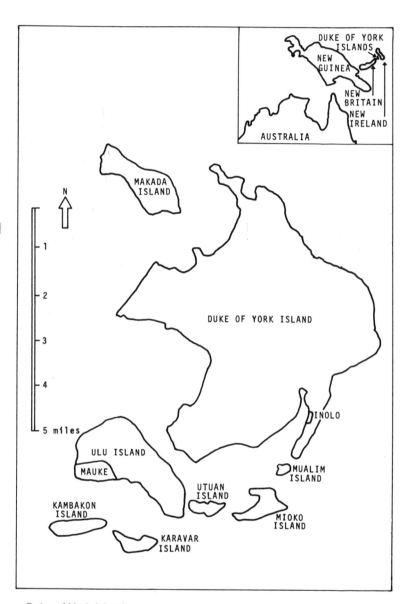

Duke of York Islands

of proper conduct. In the momboto, the Karavarans say, men looked and behaved like wild animals. They did not shave or cut their hair; they had red eyes "like wild pigs"; they were cannibals and ate even those now considered to be their kinsmen as though their kinsmen were animals. There was no kinship; there was no regulation of sex. Men had sexual relations with women who would now be considered their sisters or sisters' daughters; men did not purchase brides nor did they pay adultery fines. In the absence of regulation, men simply fought each other to get women. Their image of the momboto is a statement of the Karavaran view of basic human nature, a nature of greed and violence, characterized by the untrammeled exercise of individual interest. The expression of unrestrained human nature is seen as a chaos of conflicting desires and activities. The Karavarans refer frequently to the momboto in conversation with each other and with me.

The momboto, as an image of disorder, tells the Karavarans about the nature of order. The momboto is the reference point which shows indirectly the principles on which their current society rests. What has changed since the momboto is not human nature itself but the means by which human nature can be regulated and social order thereby established.

The momboto, in the Karavaran view, ended a few days after the arrival of George Brown, a Methodist clergyman who was the first missionary to settle in this area.[1] It is said that when he first arrived he saw that those on shore wanted to spear him; consequently he and his companions stayed on

[1] Brown established himself on the largest island (Duke of York Island) in the Duke of York group in 1876. He then moved to New Britain's neighboring Gazelle Peninsula.

their boat singing hymns continuously for three days. At the end of that time he dipped his hand into the sea. The water had been hot when he arrived but now it was cool; this indicated that the passions of those on shore had been cooled. Brown went ashore, no longer afraid. With his arrival the momboto ended and the modern era began.

Specifically, Brown and the other Europeans—all of whom are seen as arriving at virtually the same time—ended the momboto by bringing to the Duke of York Islands *divara* (shell money) and the principle of moiety.

Divara is the only indigenous Karavaran valuable. Used for both domestic purchases and ceremonial exchanges, it is made from small cowry shells (*Nassa camelus*), strung by either men or women onto thin strips of cane. Because the shells do not originate in the Duke of York Islands or in the immediately adjacent areas of New Britain and New Ireland, the supply is limited. They may be obtained through purchasing minor trade goods such as tobacco and biscuits with Australian cash (usually derived from the sale of copra) and then selling these trade goods in the village for divara. Or Australian cash can be directly converted into divara. Some Karavarans acquire divara by selling local produce such as peanuts or taro elsewhere in the Duke of York Islands. Others earn it by building canoes or providing ritual services. Most divara is acquired, however, through exchanges at marriage, mortuary ceremonies, and other ritual occasions.

Divara is measured on the body in standard lengths. One such measurement is a loop of divara running from the hand of an outstretched arm to the center of the chest and back to the hand. Following the term used by writers on the Tolai, I refer to such a length as a fathom. Divara is the single standard by which everything and everyone can be assessed and distinguished. The differences in the amount of divara that an individual owns and uses in public ceremonies distinguish "big men" from respectable followers and respectable followers from men of no consequence.[2] Divara is fundamental to the prestige system and to the ordering of society.

Moiety, say the Karavarans, was introduced with Christianity. The moieties are matrilineal and exogamous. Each moiety constitutes the outer limit of matrilineal kinship and is the only unit of kinship in which membership is determined by the absolute criterion of birth. The moieties are named after two kinds of birds: Pikalambe and Maramar.[3]

The Karavarans see their society as resting on divara and moiety, which domesticate the disruptive human energy and turn it into orderly channels. Momboto is not, however, just a state or event in the past; it is an ever-present condition of humans. The momboto in humans provides both the energy on which social forms rest and the energy which threatens to destroy social forms. This energy cannot be suppressed, but when controlled by divara in the context of moiety, it is channeled into the social forms of marriage, kinship, and politics.

Even with divara and moiety, social order seems precarious. A Karavaran told us of how enraged they had been at their treatment by a European plantation manager, suggesting that if such treatment continued, their momboto natures could not be restrained and the momboto would return.

The Karavaran view that order comes from constraint of

[2] As in many parts of Melanesia, the Karavaran term for a man of first importance is literally "big man" (*ngalana muana*); the usual term for a man of no consequence in Karavar is "man nothing" (*muana biaku*), or the same idea may be expressed merely by a contemptuous snort.

[3] The association of the moiety names with birds did not have any importance at the time of our field work. These same named moieties are found in New Britain and New Ireland, as well as throughout the Duke of York Islands.

momboto nature by divara in the context of moiety is not a view which sees social order as resulting from an interconnected and enduring system of social structure. Such analytic distinctions as office, status, rule, and norm do not reflect the Karavaran view of the basis of the order of their own society. To be sure, "office," "status," "role," "norm," and so on, are categories of anthropological analysis, and few if any tribal societies actually talk about themselves in this abstract way, yet anthropologists often suggest that these categories do express in abstract form what a society—however unclearly—thinks about itself. Since the Karavarans do not in any respect think of themselves in such social structural terms, the abstractions that compose the traditional anthropological model of social structure are inappropriate to understanding Karavaran reality.

Significantly, Epstein, too, argues (1968) that the neighboring Tolai have no concept of office. He concludes that leadership among the Melanesian Tolai, in contrast to leadership among the African Ndembu, is provided by big men whose political power does not stem from occupancy of political office. Other anthropologists also have questioned the appropriateness of applying the classical anthropological concepts of social structure to certain societies—especially to societies in the Pacific and in Southeast Asia. Their terms of "loose structure" or of "optative structure" indicate an increasing awareness that new analytic perspectives are needed if the nature of social coherence in these societies is to be understood. But as Kirsch (1969) points out, while the term "loose structure" indicates the inadequacy of the traditional concept of structure when applied to new data, it is not in itself a theory which accounts for the new data. I would add, moreover, such terms suggest an effort to stretch and thus salvage the concept of structure rather than to develop concepts of nonstructure.

If, as I have argued, the best way to understand the logic of Karavaran society is to understand it as they do, it is essential to avoid thinking of their society in structural terms. Karavarans see order as the regulation of momboto nature—the constraint of energy—rather than as the operation of social structure. Put another way, Karavaran society should not be regarded as a lattice of structural positions. There is, for instance, no office of "big man." A big man's behavior is not characterized by the intrinsic qualities of an office but rather by the kinds of relationships that he, as an individual, is able to create: a big man is an individual who controls others.

Appropriate to this view of social relations is the Karavaran concept of kinship. Kinship is not viewed as a matter of corporate groups with a fixed membership, with leadership by a genealogically specified headman or elder. Instead, matrilineal kinship is characterized by the exercise of a big man's power over his followers. Matrilineal kinship, very broadly viewed, is the product of a big man's use of his divara to control the disruptive momboto nature of a certain number of those of his own moiety. Thus a big man's followers, because they are his followers, are his kinsmen. This intimate relationship between kinship and power will be explored later in considerable detail.

Society is then, in the Karavaran view, based on individuals as individuals (that is, not as holders of office) controlling other people through divara. It is important to distinguish this kind of power from personal power. Personal power refers to force of character or of personality and is based on a concept of person which the Karavarans lack.

Karavarans do not regard individuals as having an inviolable "inner" core of the sort that we in the West conceive our "self" to be. The Karavarans have no understanding of the self-regulation we call "character." They do not speculate about each other's motives; they do not appeal to each other's conscience.[4] An individual, in their view, is not controlled by anything resembling guilt; there is nothing corresponding to an idea of "sin." People are understood only in behavioral terms. Karavans will note that a man is a chronic gossip or cigarette smoker, but no one is interested in why he has these characteristics.

The Karavaran concept of person has two consequences: The control individuals have over others is not seen as based on attributes of personality but rather on possession of di-vara; and individuals are not regarded as operating according to internal constraints—they behave in an orderly fashion only through fear that to do otherwise will result in fines of divara or in gossip.[5] (Gossip is seen as resembling a physical force that will strike the offender and cause him illness.) Only external constraint, in their view, prevents individuals from lapsing back into the ungoverned momboto behavior of their ancestors.

In the absence of a concept of enduring structure—either of social structure or of personal character—social order lacks a clearly defined foundation. Those individuals who hold power are not clearly specified by occupancy of office, nor are the nature and the limits of their power specified by the norms which define office. As a consequence, power is seen

[4] Read (1955) describes the Gahuku Gama of the New Guinea Highlands in rather the same way.

[5] The Karavarans use the word fear (*burut*) frequently when talking about the basis of social order.

not as adhering to or defining a status. The crucial questions about social order for the Karavarans concern the regulation of power: Who are the individuals exercising power and what are the limits to their exercise of power? To phrase these questions in the Karavaran idiom of the big man: In the absence of an office called "big man," which individuals are regarded as big men? In the absence of norms defining and constraining a "big man," what limits the power a big man has over his followers and the other members of his society?

These are practical questions that concern the ways people actually deal with each other. But they are also epistemological questions that concern the coherence of the Karavaran conception of their world. In the absence of such fixed reference points as are provided by a concept of structure, "meaning" itself becomes uncertain. Since the Karavarans do not understand each other through intrinsic qualities such as might be provided by character or office, how then do they define themselves and their experience?

For the Karavarans, an individual, an activity, or a concept has meaning—is intelligible—only as it is brought into contrast with another individual, activity, or concept. Each is defined through a relationship of juxtaposition. The definition of the nature of order through its contrast with disorder—or, specifically, the definition of current social life through its contrast with the life of the momboto—is the most general Karavaran definition and sets out the broadest frame of meaning. This juxtaposition reveals that social order is achieved through the operation of divara in the context of moiety. Within this broad definition of social order are other sets of juxtaposed relationships which, too, are based on the effect of divara in the context of moiety. The most important of these include the relationship between a big man and his

followers and between males and females. What it is to be a
big man or a follower can be known only through the contrasting way in which a big man and his followers interact
with each other; what it is to be a male or a female can be
known only in their contrasting relationship. Since Karavarans do not distinguish between behavior and individual
character or between role and person, an individual is what
he does. For the Karavarans, therefore, an individual is defined as a person only through his relationships.

If Karavaran life is given both order and intelligibility
through relationships of juxtaposition, it is necessary that
these relationships themselves be bounded in some way. If,
for instance, a big man is defined through his relationship
with his followers, then the nature of this relationship must
persist if the meaning of big man (and, of course, of follower)
is to persist. What then provides the parameters of interaction so that the relationships on which social and conceptual
order rest are given form? This returns us to the consideration of limitation of power. If the power of a big man were
not limited, then the relationship between a big man and his
followers would alter in nature as a big man became more
and more wealthy. But, in fact, a big man, no matter how
wealthy, cannot exceed a certain degree of control over another: no big man can act as a tyrant over his followers. To
do so would be to act as a man of the momboto rather than as
a member of society.

The Karavarans do not view the momboto nature of
humans as having the capacity for ordering itself. They do
not view their society itself as having intrinsic order of the
sort that would be provided by a concept of social structure.
Moreover, they do not have an explicit political philosophy
that could set out the nature of social order. As a conse-

quence, if there is to be a locus of ordered reality, it must be created through ways other than through personal structure (character), social structure, or an explicit political theory. For the Karavarans, the locus of ordered reality can be known only through the specification of power. If the Karavarans are to have social and conceptual order, they must specify to themselves the medium, the context, and the limits of power.

In Part I, I will show how the principal relationships of nonritual life are generated by the interaction of momboto nature, divara, and moiety. The expression of momboto nature provides the energy on which social life is based; divara operating in the context of moiety provides the form of social life.

I will begin by discussing the constraint of vital but disruptive momboto nature by the medium of divara within the context of a single moiety. Because a big man's followers (with the limited exception of his adopted sons) are drawn only from his own moiety, big men compete for prestige and followers only within the moiety; hence it is within the moiety that individual interests are most conflicting and disruptive and the control of these interests by divara most essential. This kind of relationship characterizes matrilineal kinship.

The relationships of patrilateral kinship differ significantly from those of matrilineal kinship. Because a big man's followers are drawn only from his own moiety, men of opposite moieties do not compete actively for prestige and followers. They assume common interest rather than conflicting interest. In the absence of conflicting interests, momboto nature is dormant and divara is not used to constrain behavior. Under these circumstances, social relationships are different in quality from those existing between members of the same moiety. The problem of domestication of others—the constraint of their momboto nature—is no longer central.

After I have discussed these two models of social interaction between men—competitive and noncompetitive—I will deal specifically with the relations between males and females. These constitute a special case in the general problem of imposing order. Females are not regarded as having the same degree of momboto energy as males, and they are not seen primarily as active agents. Nevertheless they can still have a highly disruptive effect on male relations with other males. I will argue that the Karavaran awareness of the disruptive potential of females is reflected in their beliefs that sexual contact with females is polluting to males.

The intent of my argument up to this point will be to demonstrate that the important relationships of Karavaran nonritual life are based on the conjunction of moiety, divara, and momboto nature—of both males and females. However, even though nonritual life specifies the ingredients of relationships, it does not fully specify their form. I contend that Karavaran nonritual life raises certain questions concerning limits and contours of relationships. These questions are not answered within nonritual life but they are answered during ritual. The contrast between ritual and nonritual life is most clear in the contrast that the Karavarans themselves make between the nonritual court (*vurkurai*) and the ritual court (*kilung*). I will therefore conclude my analysis of Karavaran nonritual life with a consideration of the activities of the vurkurai court. This will provide a clear statement of the nature of power and the conceptual and practical problems attendant on its use.

Part II will concern the ritual activities which answer the fundamental questions about power and social order arising in nonritual life. I will begin by describing the system of ritual grades; then I will describe the sequence and significance of the activities that compose the kilung court and the mortuary rituals.

The mortuary rituals are the most important of the Karavaran ritual activities. At these ceremonies men seclude themselves from women and construct two classes of masked figures, later to be displayed in public. These are the "female" tubuan and the "male" dukduk. The tubuan is partly distinguished from the dukduk in appearance by red eyes surrounded by several concentric white circles. Only a man who has entered the final and most exclusive of the male ritual grades has the privilege of and the ritual knowledge necessary for painting the tubuan's eyes. Such a man I call an adept. When the eyes are painted, a wild spirit is recalled from its home in the sunset and installed in the eyes. At that time the tubuan is animated; it can see and is dangerous and powerful.

In contrast, the male dukduk can be constructed by virtually any adult male. Such a figure has no eyes and is not dangerous or powerful, as it is not animated by a spirit. These two figures contrast systematically with each other in the way that each is purchased, constructed, and displayed. This contrast illuminates and specifies the nature of certain relationships of power in nonritual life and it provides answers to questions raised but not answered in nonritual life—questions that must be answered if there is to be, for the Karavarans, a secure locus of ordered reality.

Since, as I have said, the Karavaran view of social reality remains implicit in their activities and beliefs, the picture of this reality which emerges in this book is necessarily of my own construction, except in those relatively few instances in which I indicate that I am presenting an explicit Karavaran analysis. Moreover, the view of Karavaran. reality which I present is a male view. Although the men offer only little social analysis, the women, as Shelly Errington and I both concluded after considerable investigation, offer virtually no analysis at all. Karavaran reality appears in most concentrated form during ritual. Since ritual is largely the monopoly of males, the conclusions I draw about the meaning of ritual—and the nature of Karavaran reality—inevitably incorporate the male perspective.

All the ceremonial descriptions which follow are based on firsthand observation made during 1968, unless I indicate otherwise. I will also indicate those cases in which the particular ritual performance that I am discussing differs in significant detail from others of the same type which I witnessed or heard about.

PART ONE

THE CONCEPT AND
EXERCISE OF POWER

CHAPTER 1

Kinship

Relations within the Moiety: Matrilineal Kinship

Most, if not all, social interaction on Karavar is understood through kinship. Kinship in its most abstract meaning is the effect of divara on momboto nature in the context of moiety: kinship terms are condensed expressions of particular interactions of divara, momboto nature, and moiety. Relations within the moiety—that is, matrilineal kinship—are characterized by the control big men exert over their followers through divara. A big man is defined by his ability to draw followers to him. He is regarded by his followers as their matrilineal senior—usually their mother's brother (see Figure 1). Because they are his followers, they are his kinsmen; they are not his followers because they are his kinsmen. For power thus to be directly translated into kinship requires both a practical and a conceptual precondition: a big man must have substantial resources of divara; and kin groups must not be regarded as fixed in membership. Anyone within a moiety is a potential follower/kinsman of a big man.

In certain contexts, the entire moiety on Karavar may act together as though it were one big matrilineal group. On the occasion of a dukduk and tubuan ceremonial, for instance, a moiety will be at least briefly under the direction of one of its most important men. A really big man such as Alipet on Karavar—who was both the most important ritual adept and

35

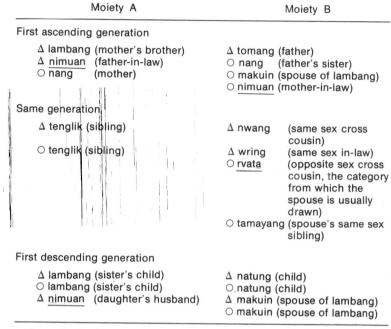

Moiety A	Moiety B

First ascending generation

Moiety A	Moiety B
Δ lambang (mother's brother)	Δ tomang (father)
Δ <u>nimuan</u> (father-in-law)	○ nang (father's sister)
○ <u>nang</u> (mother)	○ makuin (spouse of lambang)
	○ <u>nimuan</u> (mother-in-law)

Same generation

Moiety A	Moiety B
Δ tenglik (sibling)	Δ nwang (same sex cross cousin)
○ tenglik (sibling)	Δ wring (same sex in-law)
	○ <u>rvata</u> (opposite sex cross cousin, the category from which the spouse is usually drawn)
	○ tamayang (spouse's same sex sibling)

First descending generation

Moiety A	Moiety B
Δ lambang (sister's child)	Δ natung (child)
○ lambang (sister's child)	○ natung (child)
Δ <u>nimuan</u> (daughter's husband)	Δ makuin (spouse of lambang)
	○ makuin (spouse of lambang)

Figure 1. Kinship terms. This chart covers all terms of kinship address which are used by males in the three generations shown. All are declined to mean "My X" and all are extended classificatorily. Terms which must be used because personal names are prohibited are underlined. The same terms are used by a female except that she would call her sister's children "natung" and her father-in-law "tumbung" (grandfather).

the wealthiest man—is often in this context mother's brother to his moiety as a whole.[1] Although all members of a given moiety are thought ultimately to be matrilineal kinsmen, there are no myths that give circumstances of common origin nor is there any all-embracing genealogical system.

In most circumstances, however, the important kinship/political groups are smaller than the moiety. These are of two sorts: the *liting* and the *apik* (sometimes called *vuna-*

---

[1] I have used actual names throughout in the belief that the Karavarans with their emphasis on individual achievement would prefer that I did so.

tara). The liting consists of fifteen to thirty men, women, and children who consider themselves to be close matrilineal kin, although the genealogical links cannot always be demonstrated.

Everyone belongs to a liting. In some cases litings may combine to form a larger group called apik under the leadership of a big man. What determines whether a liting remains a liting or becomes part of an apik is the importance within the liting of the males of the senior generation—the classificatory or actual mother's brothers. If the liting does have an important senior male, then it may remain distinct as a liting and provide the base for his ambition. If such an individual is not present, then the liting may become part of an apik under the leadership of a big man.

This presence of a big man serves to organize people into an apik. The apik has a name only in reference to the big man, as in "Alipet's apik." A big man's following includes the members of his own liting, but to be a big man he must induce members of other litings to join with his own to form an apik. Two questions may be asked here: Why do individuals as individuals or a liting as a group attach themselves to a big man and thus move into an apik? What are the social mechanisms whereby such a transition is made in kin group membership? The answer to the first question concerns the Karavaran view of social obligation and individual worth that makes necessary a tie with an influential mother's brother. The answer to the second concerns the Karavaran view of kinship and the way in which it can be used so that lesser individuals can acquire an influential mother's brother, and influential men acquire a following of sister's sons. In the movement from liting into apik, the flexibility inherent in the Karavaran view of kinship becomes especially important.

Karavarans realize that each individual will in the course of his life have obligations to expend divara which he alone will find difficult or impossible to handle and which if ignored will bring him public ridicule and subsequent shame. Most of these obligations concern mortuary matters, which are the primary responsibility of close matrilineal kin. A man is obligated to finance the funeral of his mother, brother, mother's brother—that is, his very close liting mates with whom the actual genealogical ties are known. One of the characteristics of a big man is that he provides both leadership and divara for his matrilineal kin in these affairs, and the more important a big man is, the larger will be his group of effective matrilineal kinsmen. An apik, in fact, is explicitly defined by the Karavarans as a group pulled together by a big man's divara to perform mortuary ceremonies.

Because big men are leaders of apiks they are often referred to as *tene marmari*, or men of compassion. I suspect that this term derives from the way in which they create social order through using their divara to create a following. As the force which is seen to constrain the selfish nature of others, big men, by contrast, should be regarded as compassionate.

During our 1968 study, Ambo was an aspiring big man who was eager to attract new supporters, expand his influence on Karavar, and extend his reputation abroad. He was therefore particularly generous to his followers in order to attract more of them. For instance, an insignificant mother's brother of Daki, one of Ambo's young followers, died. As the genealogically nearest adult male matrikinsman, Daki was primarily responsible for the funeral proceedings. Ambo was enormously helpful to him in making proper arrangements, in giving advice on protocol, and in generously contributing divara and money to the ceremony. All this assistance enhanced Ambo's prestige as a wealthy, generous, and compassionate man. The ceremony did not much enhance Daki's prestige, but he was saved from the humiliation of sponsoring an inadequate performance.

Virtually everyone who is not a big man in his own right, or at least important, feels that he will need the help of a big man in meeting such obligations. Such men become bound to a big man in the anticipation of future need. Certain young men who need help in arranging their marriages may become even more dependent on a big man.

Most marriages are within the community. Marriage arrangements require that the bride price be borrowed from a number of people—even sometimes from the bride's kinsmen—by someone other than the groom. The groom's sponsor, usually a man, who solicits these loans, guarantees their repayment. Shortly after the bride price has been accepted by the bride's party, usually by her father, the various loans are paid back by this sponsor. In effect the sponsor consolidates the debt and the groom owes only his sponsor rather than the large number of people who had earlier cooperated. If a prospective groom's father is living, he will almost always sponsor his son, and furthermore, he will not expect repayment. However, if the father has died or if the groom is still a young man and has already lost one or sometimes several bride prices provided by his father in unsuccessful marriages, someone other than the father will act as sponsor. Thus, if for any reason the groom's father is unable or no longer willing to collect the loans and guarantee repayment, the groom will go to a big man of his moiety in search of a sponsor.

There are several advantages to the groom in having a big

man arrange his marriage. If a young man seems unable to keep a bride, a big man through his contacts in neighboring communities may be able to acquire a bride from a place where the young man's reputation for sloth or other failings has not penetrated. (In such an arrangement the young man may marry a girl of bad reputation whose kinsmen must go afar to seek a groom.) Furthermore, since the return of the bride price in cases of divorce is not automatic, a big man has a better chance than would a lesser man of getting the bride price back in case the marriage fails.

The big man also reaps advantages: arranging a marriage gives him prominence as a man of both financial means and compassion. Moreover, the big man acquires a follower. There is a generally observed obligation on the part of a young couple to live in the hamlet of the man who has sponsored the purchase of the bride—whether the sponsor is the groom's father or a member of the groom's moiety, such as his big man.

When anyone other than the father buys the bride, the groom, as I have mentioned, is obligated to repay the debt and to live in the sponsor's hamlet until the debt to him is paid. The groom will usually work directly for the big man in order to liquidate his debt. Calculation of the debt as it is liquidated is made by the big man and is based on his appraisal of the value in divara of the groom's contributions to the big man's garden, and so forth. Not only has the big man gained a helper whose efforts in the garden will augment his own supply of divara, but he has a follower who will run errands for him, assist him in ritual affairs, and help with divara in exchanges.

A big man is often able to keep these young men of his moiety—his classificatory sister's sons—as followers even after they have paid off the bride price. They will probably no longer be expected to work in his gardens but like other followers will remain in his debt. The nature of the indebtedness is based on the way accounts are tallied. A big man's help to a follower is dramatic: Ambo, in the example just mentioned, contributed in a spectacular way with divara and leadership to the funeral Daki was obligated to sponsor. In contrast, the help that a follower gives his big man is unobtrusive—running errands, and following him in ritual activities. The outlay for many of these activities is not applied to the debt. In the act of following, a follower may expend over a period of time considerable amounts of his own divara—to say nothing of energy—which is not put into the balance against the big man's more conspicuous expenditures.

Virtually the only kind of debt that a follower will be able to pay off is the bride price. Even so the follower never knows at any time exactly how the balance of this debt stands since the big man keeps track of payments and only tells the follower when it is paid off. (In contrast, two big men who are in the midst of an exchange both know exactly what the debt is and on what occasion it will be repaid. This is a relationship that can be terminated.) Furthermore, while a man acts as a follower and is represented by his big man, his debt increases. Thus the generosity of a big man, by which he wins public approval as a man of wealth and compassion, can also be viewed as the lure which attracts followers into the sticky web of perpetual obligation.

A big man's relationship to his followers may change over the years. At first when a big man is trying to expand his following, he is likely to present himself as generous and compassionate. After his prestige is firmly established, the emphasis may change: he may demand more and more from his followers, who are by now much indebted to him. Alipet, for instance, at first had a reputation of being good to his followers but later became autocratic and quick to anger. Both of these characteristics are regarded as usual in well-established big men. I suspect that quick anger is used by big men as a symbol of their importance to show that they need not fear any consequences of their anger. Alipet had antagonized his young followers, although most still lived near him and continued to support him. They were afraid that if they deserted him he would demand back all the divara that he had spent for them during the time when they were bridegrooms or otherwise dependent on him. Most likely Alipet was no longer worried about increasing the number of his followers, and as long as he had divara as the basis of his power and prestige, he could maintain control over them.

Now, assuming an individual needs a big man, how does he acquire one? Or, fitting the question into a larger context: how are kinship and the current realities of power made consonant?

If the liting has a senior male who is a big man, or at least an important man, his close matrikinsmen are automatically his followers. But if such leadership is lacking within the liting, its members must look elsewhere. An individual—or in some cases a liting as a group—acquires a big man by creating a relationship with him that is expressed in kin terms.

As relationships change, kinship necessarily changes also. Except for the limited number of individuals with whom specific genealogical ties can be demonstrated, anyone can be brought into or excluded from kinship relationships. Such demonstrable genealogical ties are few: there are no coherent genealogies linking members of the same apik; few Kara-

varans remember the names of their deceased grandparents.[2]
Kinship can be asserted in several ways to express relationships such as those between a big man and a follower or
between any individuals engaged in cooperation which both
find politically advantageous.

One way to affirm kinship is simply to assert that particular members of the previous generation behaved toward each
other as kinsmen. Thus, two men may express their cooperation with each other simply by saying that their fathers cooperated in work, usually in ceremonial work. This is phrased
as *turwung ura pinepam*, which means "stand together in
work." If their fathers acted together as brothers (*dina*), so
too, their sons are brothers. This technique is generally used
to link men of the same generation, although it can be used
between men of adjacent generations. Thus a son of one of
two men who had cooperated could assert that a special relationship of father and son existed between himself and his father's partner.

Another way of asserting kinship is through what I will
call adoption. Adoption is probably the most versatile means
of expressing both new and already existing ties. More than
two-thirds of Karavaran children are adopted, although most
continue to live with and be supported by their natal parents.
Adoption expresses ties between sets of parents and provides
the adopted child when he becomes adult with a means of
expressing ties which he himself wishes to establish.

Only if the adoptive parents are childless do they assume
the full responsibilities of parenthood for the child. In these

[2] The apiks are, moreover, not related to each other by any higher order
than that of shared moiety. The genealogical knowledge that is associated
with a segmentary system is completely lacking.

cases the child is often adopted from a very close kinsman—either from a husband's brother or a wife's sister. Occasionally the child may be adopted by kinsmen living as far away as New Britain and thus be separated for long periods from his natal parents. Childless adoptive parents assume all the expenses for and have full control over the child—in ritual matters for the boy and in marriage for either a boy or girl. Such a child has the same mortuary obligations toward his adoptive parents as any child has toward his natal parents. He will, in fact, have full mortuary responsibilities toward both adoptive and natal parents, although in these cases both sets of parents may be so closely related that he will act simply in the manner expected of anyone toward his primary kin. This kind of adoption is relatively unusual; it establishes kinship obligations that cannot easily be altered.

In the usual kind of adoption the ties created are more provisional. A child of either sex can be adopted by a woman in conjunction with her husband or her brother. The more frequent of these alternatives is for a husband and wife to adopt a child—who can be of either moiety or sex—by making arrangements with its parents, often before the child is born. For example, two men of the same moiety, although unable to link each other genealogically, are considered to be brothers not only because they cooperate in ritual but also because one has adopted the other's child. The actual transfer of divara that marks the adoption may take place in several stages, and, if the two men or their wives quarrel, the adoption and with it the kinship relationship may be terminated and the divara, if already transferred, returned.

Adoption, besides expressing special kinship ties between pairs of adults, provides adopted children with many potential kinsmen. As an adult, a person can assert the existence of

certain ties that are based on his position in the kinship net-
work both of his own parents and of his adoptive parents.
The tie between his own parents and the adoptive parents
may be expressed by the assertion that his real mother and
adoptive mother were sisters, or that their mothers were sisters, so that he treats as his own close kinsmen those of his
adoptive parents. Furthermore, through the practice of adoption, a child acquires not only another set of parents but
other sets of siblings: his natal mother's adopted children; his
adoptive mother's natural children; his adoptive mother's
adopted children. As a child, he regards these as his siblings.
As an adult, he will continue to regard as siblings only those
with whom he cooperates.

Potential ties through adoption can thus be transformed
into kin ties: I asked Diul, a man about forty years old, who
had purchased his wife for him. Diul said it was Doti, a very
important man on the neighboring island of Utuan. Diul was
unable to trace his specific genealogical tie to Doti but only
asserted that Doti was his *ngala*, that is, his most important
mother's brother. In this particular case, however, Diul's
mother, Lokoko, remembered how this link of mother's
brother–sister's son had originated between Doti and Diul.

Lokoko and Doti had both been adopted by the same
woman. When Doti bought a wife for Lokoko's son Diul, the
relationship between Doti and Diul was that of mother's
brother to sister's son, based on the sibling relationship between Lokoko and Doti. I can only speculate on Doti's reason for becoming an active mother's brother for Diul. I suspect that it was because Lokoko's true brother, Kaliop
—hence Doti's adopted sibling along with Lokoko—
became a very important man himself. Doti, therefore, acted
as Kaliop's brother. After Kaliop died and Diul was ready to

marry, Doti continued in this kinship position and was the mother's brother for Diul. Presumably it will be to Diul's benefit to maintain this tie since Doti is very important.

In some cases an entire liting may follow the lead of one or several of its members and attach itself to a big man. This results in the enlargement or the formation of an apik. We were able to document one such case in which a liting brought itself into the following of a big man. The process began during the final years of a big man named Tonga, probably in anticipation of his death or political eclipse. Tonga controlled an apik composed of two litings. When he died in 1968, one of his senior classificatory sister's sons, Twembe, sponsored a particularly elaborate and expensive funeral (distinct from the mortuary ceremony which may come years later—in this case during 1972). Although the full extent of a person's wealth in divara is secret, even from a full brother, there was reason to think that Twembe was wealthy, as he had a good income from building canoes. It was further known that he was planning to purchase the rights to make a tubuan at the next opportunity so that he could act in ritual matters as a big man—an adept capable of sponsoring a mortuary ceremony. Thus Twembe was in a position to take over the two litings that were still grouped around Tonga at the time of his death.

In addition, another liting was actively trying to ally itself to Twembe. This liting was composed of a group of very close matrilineal kin for whom all the connecting links were precisely known (see Figure 2): there were two full sisters of the senior generation, Ialu and Lokoko, plus their children and the children of their daughters. In addition there were two men, Tanglik and his brother William, true parallel first cousins of Ialu and Lokoko. These two males were the unambiguous seniors in the liting and if either of them had had an

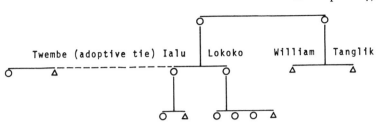

Figure 2. Twembe and Ialu's genealogy

inclination to exercise leadership over the liting he would
have had a ready-made following. William, however, the
elder of the two, lived on another island, and Tanglik was
unsuitable in that he seemed to have no ambition.

To illustrate: Tanglik neither adopted children nor offered
any of his own for adoption, This is very unusual and shows
a lack of interest in establishing or expressing social ties.
Tanglik was a failure as a liting head and was rejected by the
other members of his liting as a partner in the kinds of economic exchanges for which his position in the liting qualified
him. As evidence of this rejection, he did not receive even a
token share in the bride price of Ialu's daughter.

The overtures from this liting to Twembe's were made
primarily by Ialu, one of the two senior women and an aggressive and determined person. Even before Tonga had
died, Ialu often had one of Twembe's little daughters stay to
eat with her. Furthermore, Ialu often talked with Twembe's
sister and borrowed her children as companions and helpers.
At one point, in a quarrel with Twembe's wife, Ialu accused
her of eating up all of Twembe's food and thus of being a
parasite. Although this insult may have been tactically unsound, as Twembe was attached to his wife, it did show Ialu
conspicuously taking the perspective of a member of
Twembe's matrilineal group.

The decisive action occurred, however, when Tonga died.

Ialu went into extensive mourning as if she were one of the women of Tonga's apik and consequently a close relative of Twembe. In fact, she mourned longer than anyone except Tonga's widow. (The widow customarily has by far the longest mourning period.) The reason she gave for her extensive mourning when we asked her was that she was Twembe's sister, explaining further that Twembe's mother had adopted her to be a sister to Twembe. She was now acting as his sister. Ialu's behavior attracted the interest of other people as well and the word went around that Ialu was *waping* on Twembe. *Wap* means literally "to lean on," and in this context it meant that Ialu was in the process of acquiring Twembe as her big man. Since such a transition would probably apply to the other members of Ialu's liting, it appeared that the whole liting was in the process of placing itself under the direction of Twembe, who would then have control of a total of three litings and thus a large apik.

Ialu was capitalizing on a link through adoption: she was converting the adoptive tie into one of kinship. In time I am sure the connection between the two litings will be regarded as in fact one of genealogically demonstrable kinship. In the future it might well be said either that Ialu and Twembe were siblings or, more likely, that their mothers were sisters. It is very common for sisters to adopt each other's children, and Ialu and Twembe certainly had acted as though they were the children of sisters.

The system of kinship does present constraints which both help and hinder particular individuals in becoming important men, if not big men. Tanglik's genealogical position certainly gave him an enviable opportunity to become a big man. Twembe in contrast was forced to wait for his matrilineal senior, Tonga, to die before he could exercise his ambitions.

Yet Twembe was fortunate in that the other senior men of the litings which composed Tonga's apik—that is, Tonga's classificatory sister's sons—were almost as ineffectual as Tanglik. This system, despite such constraints, has enough flexibility so that someone else will become a leader if the senior mother's brother is not a big man. Kinship groups necessarily are a big man's following and are determined by the current distribution of power.

(Twembe will also be helped in his rise as a big man by the fact that the Duke of York ceremonial system requires that each moiety have at least one leader. Alipet clearly leads the Pikalambe moiety, but after Tonga's decline there was no one important enough to lead the Maramar moiety. Twembe was thus moving into a social vacuum, as the other important Maramar men had had static reputations for some time and appeared unlikely to have the divara and the ambition to move into the first rank. It was interesting, therefore, that after Twembe's exemplary job of sponsoring Tonga's funeral, Twembe and Alipet often sat together in conference. For Alipet, Twembe was a necessary colleague among the Maramars.)

Relations between the Moieties: Patrilateral Kinship

I have argued that matrilineal kinship is created through the use of divara: it concerns the ambivalent relationship of big men (mother's brothers) and their closely resident followers (sister's sons). This is a relationship of coercion and authority, of mortuary obligations and indebtedness. Divara provides a means of ordering the disparate private interests of men competing for prestige and power within the moiety.

Because all of a big man's following must be from his own moiety, males of opposite moieties do not compete for prestige and power. Patrilateral kinship, in contrast to matrilineal kinship, is conceptualized as following the model of the close, noncompetitive relationship between father and son.

The qualitative difference between the matrilineal and the patrilateral relationship is based on a difference in obligation to repay debts of divara. The big man's power over his followers, as we have seen, rests on their indebtedness to him. From father to son the flow of divara is not reciprocated, but in this relationship there is no obligation to repay and hence no basis for a coercive or competitive relationship.

Intermoiety relations between males are thus characterized by common rather than conflicting interest: momboto nature is less apparent in this context. Karavarans describe the close, noncompetitive tie between father and son by stating that they are "one blood" (ra gap). Although our informants would admit, if pressed, that a mother and child or father and daughter were also one blood, this idea was never spontaneously expressed.[3]

The identity between father and son, indicated by their shared blood, is a relationship between particular fathers and sons. Classificatory fathers and sons share many of these sentiments but in a less intense form. In contrast to this personal tie is the relationship between a big man and a follower. Although an actual mother's brother will have some influence over his sister's son, the real control in that son's life is exercised by his big man—either of his liting or of his apik—and

---

[3] We were unable to elicit any statements about the nature of conception or of fetal development, much less any such beliefs that were specifically relevant to the idea that father and son shared one blood. Nor could Shelly Errington get any explanation from the women about the physiological significance of menstruation, although the cessation of menstruation was regarded as a sign of pregnancy.

the big man is usually a mother's brother only in a classificatory sense.

Fathers are clearly indulgent toward their sons, especially in buying wives for them. A bride of reasonably good reputation who has not been previously married costs at least two hundred fathoms of divara, a very large sum by Duke of York standards. Some fathers had purchased several brides in succession for ne'er-do-well sons and continued to pay the adultery and other fines for their sons' misconduct well after the sons had reached adulthood. Furthermore, a father generally pays his son's entrance fees for all but the highest grade in the men's dukduk and tubuan society. Of a group of sons, the eldest is usually favored most with divara by his father, perhaps because the eldest is in turn supposed to assist his siblings after the father's death.

One example further illustrates the contrast between the relationship of father to son and mother's brother to sister's son: A few men in middle life become adepts by purchasing the right to make a tubuan and along with this right the spells that are necessary in constructing it and protecting themselves from it. In one stage of the mortuary ceremony, each ritual adept strikes his particular tubuan with a roll of divara. This is regarded as a moment of great danger to him, for unless he utters the proper spell, his tubuan will kill him. It is therefore of paramount importance that the adept learn an efficacious spell. Both the spells and the right to make a specific tubuan are usually purchased from a mother's brother who is a big man, although I was told explicitly in this connection that a man cannot always trust his mother's brother: some are well disposed and some are not. A man can, however, always trust his father. Therefore, although he will formally buy the tubuan and spells from a mother's brother, he will feel safer in using the spells given to him privately by his father, assuming his father is an adept.

The quality of the father-son tie is often the subject of spontaneous discussion. Our cook, for instance, was rhapsodizing one day about the good things of life, especially about the season when the prevailing winds switch direction. He said that at this time the whole world is lovely and fresh. The islands seem to just float on top of the water; women go slipping through the woods thinking of their husbands or lovers. Such is the time when a man thinks of his father and all the things his father has given him.

No one ever talks about a mother's brother that way.

Kinship, Inheritance, and Power

The Karavarans, then, explicitly contrast matrilineal and patrilateral relationships. The contrast between each kind of relationship is particularly apparent with regard to inheritance.

The two important kinds of inherited property are divara and the control over coconut trees. Copra is the major source of cash and cash can be converted into divara. If the estate is small and neither the sons of the deceased nor his sister's sons are men of importance, the estate is shared among them. Inheritance of these modest estates does not greatly affect current political relations, although the distribution of the estate does remind everyone that there is a division of interest between matrilineal and patrilateral sides. The most interesting cases occur when the estate is large and when one or several of the prospective heirs are already big men who almost by definition are not interested in compromise.

Whoever distributes the most divara at the funeral of a close kinsman, and thus acts as a de facto sponsor of the funeral, is able to inherit most of the estate. Since a man can inherit from the father as well as from the mother's brother, a man who is wealthy and assertive can acquire both his father's and mother's brother's estates. Furthermore, he may be directly helped in this acquisition by his father, and later he will in turn probably help his son.

Such is what happened in Alipet's case: Alipet, as may be recalled, was the most important of the Karavaran big men and controlled considerably more coconut trees than anyone else on the island. He acquired his coconut trees from three separate sources: his father, his father's brother, and his mother's brother. Alipet himself told us that he received coconut trees from his father and mother's brother. He did not mention the inheritance from his father's brother, which left hard feelings among the other rivals for the estate.

Our account of Alipet's inheritance from his father's brother came from Wilson, our cook and a member of Alipet's apik. (Although Wilson's account may not have been entirely impartial, he was a very reliable informant.) Wilson claimed that Alipet's father, Bene, was a brother of Wilson's mother's father, Tongalik. (I am not sure exactly how close a "brother" is indicated here.) Tongalik died after Bene, and Wilson said that Tongalik's coconut trees should have gone to his children—that is, to Wilson's mother and her brother—just as Bene's coconut trees had gone to Alipet. However, Alipet was already a big man when Tongalik died, and Tongalik's son, Lakur, was still young and insignificant. Alipet was therefore able completely to eclipse Lakur at Tongalik's funeral by distributing quantities of divara and thus acting as the sponsor of the funeral. Alipet in this way was able to gain control of Tongalik's coconut trees. The defeated son Lakur left Karavar in anger and settled in New Britain (see Figure 3).

In addition, Alipet had given a spectacular funeral at the

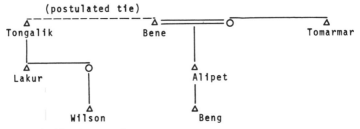

Figure 3. Alipet's genealogy

death of his own father Bene. It was one of the only two examples of a particular kind of very elaborate funeral described to us. Preceding such a funeral a tubuan figure is constructed so that it can give special attention to the dying man and then, after he has died, swish flies away from his body for a number of hours. I do not think that Alipet had any serious rivals for Bene's estate; in any case Alipet acted as only a big man could act and thus would have overwhelmed almost any rival.

I asked informants how Alipet had such a supply of divara *before* he inherited these estates. The answer was that Bene, his father, had given him divara while he was still living and, in effect, gave Alipet the advantage over Bene's own matrilineal kin. Thus Alipet cornered the estates of both his father and his father's brother. In addition, he inherited from his mother's brother, Tomarmar.

Big men usually express their wishes about the inheritance of their estates, and these wishes have some effect on the actual inheritance, especially as they concern property a man created through his own efforts. Such property might include a trade store a man had built or a stand of coconut trees he had planted. A man would wish that his son inherit this sort of property, yet even in cases of this kind such a preference would only be one of a number of factors which could influence the final distribution of the estate. It might be claimed for instance after a man's death that his trade store had actually been constructed and stocked through cash contributions of his liting and should therefore be controlled by a member of that liting, rather than by a son.

A man is even less able to control the disposition of property that he acquired matrilineally since this is thought to belong to the liting. As a consequence, the estate of a man like Alipet which came from several sources is itself likely to be split up in various ways, unless one of the potential heirs—a member of the liting or the deceased man's son—is of sufficient importance to collect the whole estate.

Alipet told us that he wanted his own estate to be distributed in the following way: the trees that he acquired from his mother's brother were to go to his matrilineal kinsmen. He wanted his son Beng to control the coconut trees that he himself had planted. But he also wanted Beng to control the coconut trees that he inherited from Bene, his own father. This was a delicate matter since Bene's coconut trees were inherited from his liting, the members of which still maintained an interest in them. Alipet circumvented this problem when talking to us by asserting that Beng was actually from the same liting as Bene. The fact was that Bene's own liting had largely died out; the only survivors were a small boy and his mother living on the neighboring island of Utuan. This boy was not likely to be important on Karavar for a number of years, if ever, and therefore probably would be squeezed out by Beng or some other big man.

Karavaran inheritance should not be viewed as the application of norms and rules concerning kinship relations. Rather, it is a process based on considerations of demography, power, and individual aspirations. These considerations lead to highly particular solutions. The Karavarans do, however, have ideas about what are ideal or normative practices concerning inheritance: there is a norm that coconut trees should remain in the liting; there is another norm which designates those who are regarded as close enough to the deceased to be potential heirs. The important point, though, is that these norms or ideals are not regarded as the foundation of society. The actual outcome of inheritance cases—or, as we will see, settlement of disputes—does not necessarily conform to these norms. Cases which do not conform to the norms are not regarded as anomalous, exceptional, or deplorable, although ill feeling may be aroused among the losers. They are regarded as entirely usual. The outcome of an inheritance case or a dispute is not a statement about norms, rules, or social structure; it is rather a statement about the interaction of various forces, the most important of which is the current distribution of power.[4]

Inheritance and kinship operate so that a man who can act like a big man—one who is politically astute in his use of divara—will acquire the additional wealth and following which will confirm him as a big man. Although a man may by virtue of a wealthy father, for instance, have a better chance than others of becoming a big man, an incompetent cannot become a big man.[5] The process of becoming a big

[4] The Karavarans realize the importance to their conceptions of social order of such a flexibility in the process of inheritance. For instance, they united in opposing efforts by the Australian administration to have their land surveyed and registered. Such registration would have rendered inheritance less suitable as one of the bases and indicators of power.

[5] There were recognized cases of men who had every possible advantage from wealthy and indulgent fathers, but who were not able to become big

man itself provides the proof that this individual can act as an established big man.[6]

---

men. The reasons for individual success or failure are not seen as reflecting differences in personal qualities nor are they usually subject to speculation.

[6] An incompetent big man is a contradiction in terms partly because the Karavarans have no concept of office, that is, of a distinction between person and office; it would not be a contradiction in terms to speak, for instance, of an incompetent king or an incompetent president.

CHAPTER 2

Male-Female Relations

Male-female relationships represent a special aspect of the Karavaran preoccupation with the domestication of their disruptive and selfish natures. Men regard female sexuality with ambivalence. Women are essential because of their capacity to bear children, but they are also threatening to social order because their sexual desirability turns men against each other. Many accounts of the momboto concern the disruptive effect of women: in the absence of moiety and divara, access to women was not regulated through moiety exogamy and bride price; there was no means of restoring peace between men through payment of divara as adultery compensation.

Even though the Karavarans believe that moiety and divara were introduced in large part to mediate male desires for women, Karavaran men continue to regard women as the source of much dissension. Women are not regarded as having the same degree of vital but disruptive energy as men have. They are seen more as desirable and elusive objects than as active agents. Consequently they cannot themselves be adequately controlled by divara, since divara can operate with full effect only as a constraint on energy. Divara is used to control male access to women rather than to control women themselves. (There are some occasions, notably the *kavei*, in which men try to induce women to come fully under the control of divara. Such efforts are not, I will indicate, regarded as generally successful.)

58

Control of male access to women is often imperfect. When the sexual desirability of women causes men to break through the constraints of divara, they revert to the chaotic behavior of the momboto by fighting or resorting to sorcery. We were often told that Karavar even in the recent past had several times the current population. The population was said to have declined because many deaths resulted from love magic and fighting over women. A man would frequently seduce a woman with love magic and then her male relatives or husband would seek revenge through sorcery or physical assault. Moreover, men are clearly aware of the bad feeling that women can cause between men by upsetting their political arrangements. Men frequently speak with feeling about the trouble women cause: a man might collect a bride price with difficulty and then the woman might run away to another man, leaving the men to quarrel about the return of the bride price.

Men confront each other with respect to women in at least two capacities: as rivals whose selfish and disruptive desires must be channeled by divara and moiety, and as equals who establish relationships of solidarity through mutually renouncing women in ritual circumstances. Male solidarity is a positive achievement for Karavaran men because it represents a triumph over their own natures, a triumph of order over the potentially recurrent anarchy of the momboto.[1]

Under circumstances in which males as a category confront females as a category, moiety becomes less important as context than it is when males define their relations with other males without primary reference to women. Males, irrespec-

[1] I do not argue that male solidarity is universally regarded as intrinsically desirable. Rather I attempt to explain why male solidarity is regarded as desirable in the Karavaran context.

tive of moiety, value solidary relations with other males because domesticated behavior is a common objective. To be domesticated is to be fully human. Such a community of interest has its image in the father-son tie, the relationship between men of opposite moieties. Comparably, when women are regarded as a category, it is their capacity sexually to subvert order that is salient to men. They are thus perceived in sexual terms and hence as members of the opposite moiety which is composed of sexually accessible women. Just as men under these circumstances appear to each other as "fathers" rather than as "mother's brothers," women appear to men as "wives" rather than as "mothers" or "sisters." Although there are ritual occasions in which "wives" may be distinguished from "mothers," these "mothers" are regarded only as exceptions to the general classification of woman.

The capacity of women to undermine order is, I suggest, reflected in the belief that contact with women is physically polluting to men.[2] This belief both reflects and supports the male belief in the importance of male solidarity.

Both men and women believe that contact with women is debilitating to men and will cause men to age quickly and to die prematurely unless protective measures are taken. One male informant compared women to a particular kind of tree that poisons smaller trees around it. Shelly Errington was told by a female informant that women were structurally unsound like the hollow papaya tree: women had a tube running from mouth to vagina. The implication was that contact with the structurally unsound women was weakening to men. In sexual contact only the man becomes polluted; his body (*pinina*) is affected by contact with a woman; the body

---

[2] Douglas (1966) discusses this same question of the relationship of concepts of sexual pollution to concepts of social order.

of a woman, in contrast, remains unchanged under all circumstances.

General contact with women, including lying on a mat that a woman has slept on or is sleeping on, is damaging to a man's health. The most acute dangers, however, come from women with whom a man has sexual intercourse because through intercourse a man may become contaminated with menstrual blood.[3]

There is an unarticulated distinction between the unconfined and polluting sexual blood of women and the normally confined, nonpolluting nonsexual blood common to both men and women.[4] Both men and women recognize that menstrual blood is particularly dangerous to men; for this reason a man cannot even wear a waistcloth that a woman has worn since it may have come in contact with her menstrual blood. Blood of childbirth, too, is dangerous to men, although this has become of little consequence since almost all births take place at the United Church hospital on the neighboring island of Ulu. However, if a woman cut her hand, for example, the blood would not be polluting to anyone.

Not only will a man prematurely age, become sick, and even die due to the debilitating effects of contact with

[3] In addition, semen loss, in the Karavaran view, if excessive, could make a man thin and weak, but this does not seem to be much of a threat in itself as occasional masturbation is considered therapeutic in the absence of other means of release. There does not seem to be a belief that sorcery is worked by the wife or her allies through semen. When I asked an informant about this possibility, he replied that if women could sorcerize their husbands then all men would have long since been dead as they frequently hit their wives and try to prevent them from running off with other men.

[4] There is no male ritualized bleeding in the Duke of York Islands as in some parts of New Guinea (see Berndt 1965:91, Hogbin 1970); furthermore, circumcision is now at least optional and is said to be done by a young man to another young man informally and without ceremony.

women, he will also become unfit company for other men. Men who spend too much time with their wives and presumably have frequent sexual intercourse with them are called *naur*, a term used with strong overtones of distaste. A naur will have dirty, dull skin rather than the clean, shining skin of a self-respecting male. One man on Karavar did spend a great deal of time with his wife, lounging around the village. Whenever my informants were discussing these beliefs with me, they would always mention him by name and express disgust at how unattractive his skin was and how old he looked.

The sexual opposition that is felt to exist between men and women has, as suggested above, a spatial analogue. The village (*taman*) is the domain of women; the men's ground (*taraiu*) is the proper domain of men.[5] The spatial opposition between taraiu and taman is part of a more extensive spatial opposition. Beyond the taraiu is the uncut forest called *lokor*. The lokor is a source of magic which a man may obtain by fasting there. Many of the spells used in constructing tubuans as well as the designs for many individual tubuans are said to have been obtained from bush spirits during these vigils in the lokor. However, such a vigil will be successful only if the supplicant has no contaminating trace of the village about him: he must have no smell of women.

Women, thus, are dangerous because they undermine both the social and the conceptual order: they cause men to behave in a disorderly way and in so doing attack the very con-

---

[5] During a flare-up of rivalry between Karavar and the nearby island of Mioko, I heard a Karavaran say that after the ritual season, the taraiu of Mioko reverted to bush through disuse. This was tantamount to insulting the Miokans by calling them a group of naurs—men who just hang about the village with the women.

cept of order itself. Men deal with this danger in several ways. One of these is most apparent in the ritual surrounding the construction of the male dukduk, during which the men seclude themselves at the taraiu. By ignoring the existence of women, the men can surmount their divisive power and create male solidarity. Another alternative employed during ritual is to domesticate female sexuality by defining women with reference to their childbearing capacity rather than with reference to their sexual desirability. These two alternatives will be discussed later. A third alternative concerns the use of a preparation called *polo*.

Polo has perhaps the most complex meaning of these alternatives: it is the most realistic of them in the sense that it contends with the full ambivalence felt concerning relations between men and women. Men cannot do without women: society needs their children—litings and apiks need members—and men, moreover, cannot fully control their own sexual desires. On the other hand, men fight over women. Women are not only essential but dangerous. This ambivalence is represented in the male preparation and consumption of polo.

Polo is a coconut oil mixture prepared informally by small groups of men, either at the men's ground or in some spot in the bush where women are unlikely to intrude. The men first make a trough of scorched banana leaves which they fill with coconut cream made by squeezing coconut water with scraped coconut. To this liquid they add hot stones. The excess fluid boils off leaving coconut oil, which is then eaten with bananas or rice.

The utensils of leaves and coconut shells are burned after the meal because anything retaining a trace of polo is very dangerous to women. I was told that if a woman were to eat from these utensils she would run sexually amok, demanding sexual intercourse from any man she encountered without consideration for incest restrictions. (Men frequently mention the sexually aggressive woman who seduces men indiscriminately: in these examples it is always she who transgresses the boundaries of proper kin behavior and has intercourse with close relatives. No opprobrium seems to fall on the men for having intercourse with a close kinswoman.)

Polo made and eaten in this rather impromptu fashion is essential to the male program of hygiene which makes the man's skin clean and body youthful, partially offsetting the effects of contact with women. Men eat polo not only to restore their health which has been undermined by contact with women but also to make themselves sexually attractive to women. Furthermore, love magic is worked through polo, especially during the *liu*—a kind of mortuary ceremony composed of dances.

Men seclude themselves for a number of days preceding the day of the liu and eat polo frequently. This polo is made in the same way as the polo taken informally as part of a program of male hygiene except that love magic spells are sometimes added. These spells suggest considerable sexual ambivalence. One spell states that the woman named should be overwhelmed by the power of this magic and leave her house compulsively seeking sexual adventure. After she has thus been made vulnerable, the speaker of the spell will swoop down and grab her like a sea eagle. During a liu, polo may also be treated with another spell that has such power that any woman a man talked to after he has eaten the polo would be seduced. Under these circumstances, a man must be careful not to talk with any close kinswoman.

Men take polo either for a liu or as normal routine in a

secluded group. This is an occasion for relaxed camaraderie, for the development of strong feelings of solidarity. All men are equally susceptible to the powers of women to pollute them and all men need to restore their health. Although polo is taken to make males sexually desirable as well as to restore male health, there is no suggestion that polo makes particular men more attractive than their fellows and thus gives them a competitive edge. Polo is associated with love magic and is itself a kind of love magic. As such it has the objective of bringing women under male control: when men take polo together they are making women in general susceptible to male charms.

Of the alternatives available to men for dealing with women, polo most accurately corresponds to the nature of Karavaran daily social life. With polo, men acknowledge the ultimate impossibility of ignoring the existence of women and of completely controlling their own sexual desires. Men thus concede that they cannot fully master their own disruptive natures, but with the use of polo, they are at least able to coexist with women without plunging back into the complete anarchy of the momboto.

CHAPTER 3

The Vurkurai Court

The central problem that the Karavarans face is to determine the locus of order. Granted that competitive relations require regulation, how is this regulation accomplished? Granted, also, that big men indeed control others with divara, what are the limitations on a big man's power? Big men are not conceived of as having limits to their control of others either through the duties of office—for the Karavarans have no concept of office—or by the restraints of character or conscience—for the Karavarans have no concept of character or conscience. Clearly, though, there must be limitations: otherwise big men would themselves not be different from men in the momboto.

Order is the direct concern of the two kinds of indigenous courts. The *vurkurai* court concerns the exercise of power; the *kilung* court concerns the constraint or limitation of power. The contrast between the two courts reflects the contrast between nonritual and ritual life. Through this contrast the questions which arise about the exercise and the constraint of power—about the locus of order—are answered.

The vurkurai is the village court which settles disputes. Anyone in the village can attend and participate. Some of the disputes are minor and are between individuals whose normal relationships are noncompetitive. In one such case a father complained about his son: the father had bought a wife for his son but his son was neither eating nor living with her and was not speaking to his father. A case may be brought forward to settle a minor marital dispute. For example, a wife complained that her husband had destroyed some of her property in anger. The expectation in disputes of this sort is that amicable relations can be restored through an admonition from the court or simply through the expression of the grievance.

In politically important disputes one side seeks to have the other fined, either in divara or in cash. One such case was brought by a big man who demanded that one of his recalcitrant followers be fined for cutting down coconut trees that each claimed as his own; another was brought by the kinsmen of a woman who demanded that she be divorced from her husband and paid damages by him because he had beaten her severely.

Individuals of either sex may submit a case to the village *luluai*. (The village luluai is a person who represents the community to the European administration.) The luluai may or may not then assemble a vurkurai. The luluai's decision whether or not to call a vurkurai often reflects his perception of the political implications of the case. If a vurkurai is assembled, accusations are made, witnesses called, debates conducted. Finally a decision may be reached—a rough consensus of the more important men present—and a fine levied on the offender or admonitions rendered. The court, however, does not have the power to make the accused come to the meeting, and often the accused simply does not come; nor does the court have the power to collect the fine.

The vurkurai court serves to crystallize social opinion, to transform diffuse gossip into social pressure and to permit participants to maneuver for support. Although the vurkurai may crystallize opinion, it does not, as mentioned, have the power to enforce its decisions. Rather, what goes on outside the court in normal life is what influences the court's decision and determines whether fines are paid, whether big men can control their followers, or whether husbands can maltreat their wives. Often those who would seemingly benefit most from a favorable consensus of the vurkurai—the weak, especially old women and young men—are those who realize that there would be little gain for themselves but considerable ill will aroused in the accused if they were even to submit their case to a court. The court, moreover, probably would not decide in their favor, but even if it did, its decision could not be enforced. If they were not, for instance, paid back a debt outside the court, it is clear that they would themselves not be able to enforce any favorable decision of the court. Usually when the court does appear to act "impartially," the case is between approximate equals.

Conversely, the court appears most "partial"—most political—in those cases between men of unequal importance. Big men bring suit against lesser men in the vurkurai, although the reverse would never happen. Because big men have power in social life outside the vurkurai court, they are assured a favorable decision inside the vurkurai court. A favorable decision can only reflect and augment their prestige, and they know, furthermore, that their own influence will be sufficient to enforce the court's decision. The following example of such a case between Alipet, a big man, and Koniel, a man of lesser importance, illustrates the essentially political nature of the vurkurai court.

A review of Alipet's political position may be helpful. Alipet was the most important man on Karavar: he was the wealthiest in divara and in cash; he was the senior and the most important of the Karavaran ritual adepts. Some years before he had been widely known for his generosity to his young followers. They spent their leisure time in his company, took their meals at his house, and worked for him in his gardens. By the time of the suit, however, Alipet had become more interested in exploiting his followers than in acquiring new ones. His joviality had become transformed into a rather arrogant and autocratic domination of dependents. As a result of Alipet's new mien, several of his followers had moved to other islands to get away from him, and none of those who remained was willing to work in his gardens.

Koniel was one of these young followers. He was something of a nonconformist, choosing to be a Seventh-Day Adventist on an island where everyone else was affiliated with the United Church. His religious affiliation made him conspicuous because he did not smoke or chew betel nut. Perhaps his outstanding social characteristic was that he had no close relatives on Karavar and few even in the Duke of York Islands. His father had married in from New Britain and his Karavaran mother's liting was virtually extinct. After the death of his parents, he was almost without Karavaran kinsmen. At the time of our study, he was rather desperately using all possible ties through adoption and common residence to claim kin relationships. Because he had worked for Europeans for a number of years, he was, for a young man, wealthy in cash. He was ambitious and enterprising, a man whose wealth—since cash can always be converted into shell money—might make him a threat to the existing power holders. In short, not only was he rather pushy, but he had no close kinsmen whose good will he could rely on for support. Koniel's position was precarious.

Alipet had the vurkurai convened in order to fine Koniel for cutting down some of Alipet's coconut trees. This case can be viewed as Alipet's effort to squash a potentially rebellious follower at a time when his other followers were squirming under his domination.

What follows is a transcription of the vurkurai:

Alipet: Before, there were twenty trees. Koniel cut down seven of them.

Koniel: I was confused. Anyway I only cut down three coconut trees and they were dry and not doing well. I meant to tell you but I had to go away and didn't return until late Sunday night. On Monday morning I heard that you had already placed your complaint with the luluai so I didn't tell you then.

Alipet: None of those trees were sick—all were fine.

Aping (the assistant luluai):
           Don't cut first and then ask; ask first. The person who planted it should then cut it himself and you will know that he agrees to have it cut.

Alipet: Koniel, you repudiate me. Who showed your boundaries to you?

Koniel: Misitil [Koniel's father's sister's son who lived on a neighboring island].

Alipet: He doesn't live here and I do. Now Wilson [a young follower of Alipet], for instance, approached me to see if he could plant some coconuts because he knows that I know the boundaries. Furthermore, I don't want a house there at all. You will pay for all the damages.

Koniel: I didn't know the trees were yours.

Alipet: You will pay for them all. Your father is a man from Lendip [a village on New Britain some distance away].

Koniel: That is true; have compassion for me.

Alipet: That is impossible. Wilson is a good young man but you are not. I have marked you; you are not a good man; you are only a young man [i.e., of little importance].

Aping: Koniel, you didn't ask first; that is not good. True, you and Misitil are cross-cousins but he doesn't live here and he isn't of importance to you in this matter.

Tombar (the luluai):
          Misitil misled you.

Alipet: Brother [addressing Tombar with the kinship term of solidarity], I want him to pay for the whole thing. I don't need coconuts but I am a human being like you.

Tombar: Koniel, what do you think of Alipet's talk?

Ambo (another important senior male):
          Koniel knew what he was doing.

Aping: Alipet shows the boundaries; he will teach us all; both Koniel and Misitil were wrong. Alipet is our boss and here we should respect him.

Tombar: Koniel, you will pay a fine of ten dollars.[1] (Sounds of agreement from the other important men.)

Aping: Besides, if there is this sort of fight later and there is no fine now, people will say there was no order [vurkurai—literally control, regulation, order] then.

Tombar: If someone steals then that is a ten dollar fine. Alipet, you didn't tell us the price but we think that ten dollars is fair.

[1] All sums referred to in this book are in Australian dollars.

Koniel handed over the very heavy fine of ten dollars to Tombar who then passed it to Alipet. The vurkurai went on to other matters.

In this encounter between Alipet and Koniel, Alipet asserted his prestige to the fullest. Koniel, as a man without real influence, stood no chance at all of winning the case. Alipet flatly asserted that all of the trees were his, that they were all in good health, and that seven of them, not three, had been cut. He clearly expected his word, not Koniel's, to be taken as fact. No effort was made to determine what the physical facts of the matter were, although the court could easily have visited the area where Koniel had cut down the trees and counted the stumps. Such an investigation, we were told, never takes place. The important considerations in a vurkurai are not the "facts" of the matter but the social position of those involved in the case. Recourse to "facts" would only constrain the political activity that takes place in the vurkurai.

I have suggested that the real source of the dispute was that Koniel with his resources of cash had been acting as a prospective big man, rather than as a docile follower. This was made evident when Alipet denied Koniel's importance during the vurkurai by saying, "I have marked you; you are not a good man; you are only a young man." In contrast to Koniel, Wilson was the model of a good follower, at least for the purposes of this vurkurai.

The only ones, excepting Koniel, who spoke at the vurkurai were important men of the senior generation. All of them backed up Alipet, completely closing ranks against Koniel. From a Western legal perspective, a big man, simply because he was a big man, winning a decision over a less important man might seem a miscarriage of justice. But to the

Karavarans such a decision is morally right, since it is an en-
forcement of order. As Aping said, "If there is this sort of
fight later and there is no fine now, people will say there was
no order then." The revolt of a follower against a big man is
in effect a revolt against the principle of order itself. Big men
have divara and it is right and necessary for them to control
people. Otherwise there could be no society at all.

That is not to say, of course, that Karavarans lack norms.
They recognize that they must conduct their lives according
to some pattern; hence they have rules about the range of
bride prices, and about the amount of compensation to be
paid if blood is drawn in a fight, and so on. As in Western
legal cases, the settlement of any particular case may or may
not be strictly in accordance with these rules. But a fundamental difference between Western and Karavaran concepts of "law" or "order" lies in the fact that Karavarans do
not identify the rules themselves as the major source of
order.

The great diversity of customs and rules in even closely
related neighboring groups in New Guinea is well known,
and instances have been reported by some observers of
change in rules which in anthropology are traditionally considered rather fundamental. Pospisil, for instance, reports
that a big man changed a rule of incest (Pospisil 1958:165);
shortly before our arrival on Karavar, a big man had been
able successfully to change a rule concerning the distribution
of bride price. It would seem from the apparent ease with
which rules are changed in Melanesia that Melanesians generally do not equate the code of law with order.

The Melanesian perspective contrasts with that of Aristotle in the *Politics* (Aristotle 1961:73). Concerning the wis-
dom of changing laws he says that, although in its operation

a new law may well be superior to the old one, we should carefully consider whether the mere fact of changing the law will have deleterious effects on the common man, who will perceive that law and, hence, order in society are not absolute. Such an attitude would be incomprehensible to Karavarans who never equated order with a code of law in the first place and who feel that norms can be changed with impunity.

Karavaran big men, then, have a great deal of power: they control social life, control the vurkurai court, and can change laws. But is their power unlimited? Obviously it is not. It is theoretically possible, though in practice unlikely, that an individual who happens to be a big man might physically fight with his followers; but such action would be regarded as "the momboto coming up again," rather than as a legitimate and logical extension of the powers of a big man. This idea contrasts with the Western notion of the tyrant who can order his subordinates executed or imprisoned as a natural extension of his personal power. Such a notion is inconceivable in Karavar. An attempt to control or restrain people through sorcery or spears or guns or other forms of violence is not encompassed in their notion of power. It would be seen as the expression of momboto nature.

The power of the vurkurai court is limited in the same way as is the power of the big men who dominate the court. The "settlement of disputes" in the vurkurai court depends on the political relations and relative power of the disputants rather than on the "rule of law" or the "norms." Important men control less important ones through divara, and the vurkurai is a forum and agent of power rather than a presumed impartial observer standing outside conflict and social process in order to judge it. It cannot enforce its decisions, other than by the normal political process of which it is indeed a part. It cannot kidnap defendants to ensure their presence at court. It cannot jail those it considers guilty; it can only fine them. It cannot torture defendants or witnesses to make them speak.

The limitations of power that are apparent in the activities of the vurkurai court and of the big men who dominate it stem from the limitations present in the nature of divara, the medium through which power is expressed. But, it may be asked, why do big men not redefine the medium of power so that divara could be used with fewer limitations? Why also do big men not express their power in ways other than through divara? Why, in other words, do they accept divara with its present limitations as the sole medium of power? The answer lies in the relationship established during ritual between a big man—as well as the other members of society—and the figure of the tubuan. The nature of this relationship is most evident in the kilung court, a court considered to be under the jurisdiction of the tubuan rather than under the jurisdiction of big men or of the luluai. In the kilung court the power of the tubuan is presented as the ultimate reference point of power. It is a power that exceeds and circumscribes the power of big men and hence the power exercised in nonritual life.

An analysis of dukduk and tubuan ritual follows. This ritual provides the Karavarans with the image of an ultimate order that their nonritual life requires for its achievement of a relative order.

PART TWO

THE RITUAL FOUNDATIONS OF THE CONCEPT AND EXERCISE OF POWER

CHAPTER 4

Ritual Grades

Those who participate in the dukduk and tubuan ritual have entered into a sequence of ritual grades. This sequence is one of increasing differentiation. In the first four of the ritual grades a male is differentiated from females by his incorporation into a male community; in the fifth and final grade a male is differentiated not only from females but from most other males.

The sequence begins when a boy is first taken to the men's ground. The men's ground, called taraiu, is a protected and particularly shady, sandy beach some four hundred yards long and one hundred yards deep. It is prohibited to all but those males who have been formally taken there. The taraiu is subdivided into smaller areas, each called taraiu, that are considered the property of particular litings. Access to any part of the entire taraiu area, however, is free to anyone who is permitted to go to the taraiu at all. The taraiu is not only the center for ritual activities, it is a favored spot for discussions, conversations and loafing.

The symbolism of differentiation is overt at the time that a boy first visits the taraiu. The boy is hidden by the women in the village, the domain of women and children. Women defend the boy with sticks and shouts against the male attackers. Eventually the men are able to carry the boy off to the taraiu where he remains for several weeks. This begins the process of his induction into a male community.

The next ritual grade in his progression is called "seeing the tubuan." In this stage a major male secret is disclosed: the tubuan figure removes its headdress and thus reveals to the boy that the costume comes apart and that it contains a human being. Sometime later the same sort of disclosure is made with the dukduk, the other ritual figure, showing that it, too, comes apart and has a human carrier inside. For the boy, this information is a prerequisite for ritual participation at the taraiu, either as a member of a work crew that constructs or carries such a figure, or, later in life, perhaps as one who sponsors and supervises the construction of a dukduk or a tubuan. Once a boy has gone to the taraiu, it is inevitable that he "see" the tubuan and the dukduk. These three steps are linked, are inexpensive, and are necessary for minimal ritual participation.

The next major step, called "buying the dukduk" (*kip a dukduk*), involves considerable expenditure of divara. In buying a dukduk a young man acquires copyright to a particular pattern of dukduk.[1] This stage is as far as most men go. In order to become a big man, however, it is necessary to become a ritual adept by completing the next and last stage.

Completion of the last stage, called "buying a tubuan" (*kip a tubuan*) gives a man exclusive ownership rights to a particular pattern of the tubuan and the ritual knowledge necessary to construct it. He is then in a position to sponsor a mortuary ceremony through which he can achieve renown. A person who has purchased a tubuan is called a *tene dukduk* [2] (liter-

[1] There are dozens of patterns of both dukduks and tubuans. New patterns are designed all the time.

[2] The term dukduk can refer to both dukduk and tubuan figures. In its most general reference it means "masked figure." The Karavarans, for instance, refer to the Chinese New Year dragon made in Rabaul as a dukduk.

ally, man of the dukduk), and of these adepts the most distinguished is called *tene tubuan* (man of the tubuan).

The significance of buying the dukduk can be understood only in contrast to buying the tubuan. With these latter two stages, the very simple opposition between men and women that was established in the first three stages (going to the taraiu, seeing the tubuan and seeing the dukduk) is elaborated. The more complex questions about the limits of power and the use of the two models of male-to-male relationships—noncompetitive as in the father-son tie and competitive as in the mother's brother-sister's son relationship—are confronted in the buying of the dukduk and the tubuan.

Ritual categories are clearly defined and members of one grade must not presume upon the prerogatives of the next grade. The emphasis on categories, distinctions and orthodoxy in ritual differs from the concerns of nonritual life. I have argued that nonritual life—as shown perhaps most clearly in the proceedings of the vurkurai court—is not based on concepts of status and office and, although there are norms, they are regarded neither as immutable nor as the foundation of order. The ritual grades are significant because they are purchased with divara; the differentiation created by these ritual grades is a statement of the capacity of divara to differentiate—that is, to impose order. The system of ritual prerogatives is binding on all, irrespective of degree of individual power: all are equally subject to the control of divara. There is no other medium for maintaining order.

Ritual orthodoxy is maintained in the kilung court. All males who are permitted to go to the taraiu can attend these courts and anyone present can speak. The final judgment of this court is made by the adepts, and in particular, the tene tubuan. The fines called *kilung*, as is the court itself, are always in divara and are divided among all men present, with the largest portions going to the adepts.

There will be several references to the kilung court in the following discussion of ritual grades. Since the court is considered the agent of the tubuan figure, a full understanding of the court is not possible until the meaning of the tubuan figure has been explored.

The First Visit to the Taraiu

The timing of a boy's ceremonial entry into the taraiu depends on several considerations. He must have a sponsor, often his father, who will purchase with cash such foods as rice, taro, and tins of beef, and purchase with divara such locally collected foods as fish, sweet potatoes, and bananas. In addition, the sponsor will distribute divara to the men of the community. The boy's trip to the taraiu requires, then, a certain amount of preparation. Karavarans say that usually only the boy's natal father will take these ritual duties to heart and see that the boy goes at the earliest time. Thus, a boy whose father has died and who must rely on a stepfather or adoptive father or on a mother's brother or a brother may sometimes have to wait until he is in his teens before he is taken to the taraiu.

A decision as to when the boy should go may be modified or hurriedly made if the boy breaks some of the ritual rules. During our 1968 study on Karavar only one boy was taken to the taraiu—a boy of about ten. Neither he nor his older brother had yet gone to the taraiu because their natal father had died and their stepfather, Topalangut, was a person of little wealth or drive and had not made arrangements. He was stirred to action, however, when the younger of these boys, Topap, unwittingly trespassed on a temporary men's ground where a tubuan was being constructed. The fine for an uninitiated male going on the taraiu is sixty fathoms of divara, a very substantial amount. Rather than pay this fine the stepfather quickly took the boy formally to the taraiu. In effect his privileges to go there freely were extended retroactively. The expenses incurred in this ritual were less than the sixty-fathom fine and would in any case have had to be assumed at some time in the future.

The events did not follow the standard order in one respect, since the procedure was rushed to avoid the fine. Immediately after the offense, Topalangut distributed about twenty fathoms of divara to all the men who had assembled at the taraiu. As is usual in ritual distributions, the adepts received larger shares and got their shares first. Meanwhile, Topap, the errant youth, had returned to the mission school on the neighboring island of Ulu and was not present. Several weeks later, during the school vacation, Topap returned home and was then taken to the taraiu. Under normal conditions the divara would have been distributed at this time.

On the day Topap was to be taken to the taraiu, he was hidden by the women in one of the village houses. The women, armed with stout switches, were patrolling the borders of the village awaiting the young men who would come to abduct Topap. Shelly Errington, who was with the women, was told, "This isn't a joking matter. Strike them hard!" The men came and eventually, after a good deal of skirmishing, discovered the house where Topap was hidden and carried him off to the taraiu amid furious slashing by the women. Topap, by undergoing a spatial transition from the village to the taraiu, was at the same time undergoing a social transition. He was being differentiated from women, even though he was not yet fully a male as far as participation in ritual was concerned. The women energetically expressed their opposition to the loss of one of their group.

Once at the taraiu, Topap, escorted by the young men who had abducted him, toured the individual taraius of the various litings. As they paraded through each of these, the entire group was hit on their backs by the older men who had remained at the taraiu. Being struck in this way is called *balilai*, a general term representing submission to the authority and discipline of the figure of the tubuan and of senior males, especially the adepts. My informants said that Topap and his escorts were struck because Topap was seeing these taraius for the first time. When a boy ritually sees a dukduk and tubuan for the first time he is also struck.

A further instance of balilai occurred during this tour of the taraius. One man, a volunteer, not otherwise important in this ritual, lay on his stomach without his waistcloth in order to expose his anus to the boy. An informant of sixty said that in the past a boy going to the taraiu for the first time had to perform fellatio on one of the adult men. Another informant, a young man about thirty-five, was shocked when I asked him about this practice, saying that he had never seen nor heard of such a custom.[3] He said that the boy's kinsmen would not tolerate it, because a penis that has been in contact with a vagina would poison the boy. In any case the incident that actually occurred when Topap went to the taraiu and the event alleged to have taken place in the past are both of the same order, suggesting homosexual submission when a boy is separated from the society of women and incorporated into the society of males.

Topap and his escort finally arrived at the taraiu where

[3] Parkinson (1907:544) mentions practices of sodomy in the initiation of youths into the male Iniet society among the Tolai of New Britian.

his two mother's brothers and his stepfather, Topalangut, had made minor preparations earlier during the day. Topap was seated in the center of a circle of men who watched as he ate alone from rice and tinned meat provided by his stepfather. A young man was told to sit in the center with Topap so that Topap would not be afraid and would be able to eat with a good appetite. Topap did, however, remain nervous. After his solitary meal, Topalangut paid divara to the two men who had actually entered the house where Topap was hidden and to the man who had displayed his anus. This payment followed standard procedure. If the normal pattern of going to the taraiu had been followed—if Topap had not gone in such a rush to avoid the fine—the distribution of divara by Topalangut to all the men would have taken place at this time.

For the next several days Topap stayed at the taraiu and did not go into the village at all. During this time he did light tasks such as washing out pots and other chores that boys are expected to do. According to my best informant, Topap should have been treated as a big man and should not have been required to do any work at all; in fact, he should have been waited on by his stepfather and given any sort of food that he asked for. Supposedly failure to treat the boy as though he were a big man would ordinarily be punished by fines, levied by the adepts. That was not the case in this instance, however.

The food Topap ate was cooked entirely by men at the taraiu—the only circumstance when food eaten at the taraiu must be cooked by the men there. On all other occasions food may be cooked by the women in the village and then taken to the taraiu. Once the food has gone to the taraiu, however, it usually does not go back into the village.

The day before Topap returned to school, the final phase of the ceremony took place, after which he was ready to emerge again into normal society.

In the late afternoon virtually all the males on the island qualified to go to the taraiu assembled there. Topap and several other youths—all had previously gone to the taraiu but had not yet bought the dukduk—were gathered into a group of novices called a *kamba vanai*. They ranged from about six to sixteen years of age and some had been going to the taraiu for a number of years. These youths, led and followed by an adult, went forth in a procession from the taraiu into the village and traversed the main path connecting the various hamlets. The purpose of this expedition, I was told, was to show Topap again to the women from whom he had been kept since the time of his abduction. When they came to the house where Topap and his parents lived, his mother came forward with three fathoms of divara and gave this in Topap's name to the adult leading the procession of youngsters. Another contribution of divara was given by Topap's mother's brother's wife, who was contributing for her husband. The older boys of the group were meanwhile trying to be blasé and were spitting out their saliva in the fashion of the adult betel nut chewers.

The expedition then returned to the taraiu where the divara thus collected was laid down near the food supply that had been prepared during that day. The rest of the men came forward, led by Topap's two mother's brothers, his stepfather, and stepfather's father, and threw lengths of divara on the ground on top of the two earlier contributions from the village. This divara was to be saved for Topap by his stepfather and used later when he purchased a dukduk.

The men then ate fish, bananas, and taro served with coconut sauce, all provided by Topalangut and his brothers-in-law (Topap's two liting mother's brothers). Topalangut was helped without pay in the cooking by his father, both paternal half brothers, and his two brothers-in-law. The bilateral composition of this group is typical of most work groups. The seating for the meal was similar to the seating at Topap's first meal at the taraiu, that is, men in a circle with Topap in the center; but in this case everyone ate, not just Topap. There was still a spatial distinction between Topap and the rest of the men, indicating, I was told, that he was still a *vanai* (novice). A male is in certain respects considered to be a vanai until he buys a dukduk, a ceremony which may not take place for a number of years after he first goes to the taraiu.

The events when a boy goes to the taraiu signal his separation from the company of women and his integration into the company of men. I had been told prior to the event that the women would wail loudly as Topap was taken away; they did not, although they did defend the village and its member, Topap, with considerable vigor. Topap himself seemed somewhat afraid and cried a bit at the taraiu. This behavior is considered only natural; Karavar has no cult of stoicism. Topap was not singled out for any hazing, however, even though he and his escort of young men were all swatted as they visited the various taraius. One of my informants, as I mentioned, was rather surprised when I told him that I had seen Topap working during his seclusion at the taraiu, saying that he should be treated at this time as a big man. This was "his day" (*nuna bung*). Despite lapses from this ideal, there did seem to be an effort to treat the boy very well, perhaps so that he would learn to find fellowship in the company of men. Once a boy has been to the taraiu he may go there freely, except when a tubuan is under construction, and take at least a peripheral part in the leisure activities and the discussions there.

Seeing the Tubuan and Dukduk

Usually when a tubuan is made, all the boys who have gone to the taraiu but have not yet "seen the tubuan" will take this opportunity to enter into the next stage in their ritual progression. Until this time the boys are, in theory at least, as ignorant as the women about the principal male secrets concerning the construction of the masked dukduk and tubuan figures. The men consider that the principal secret to be kept from the women is the way a man "goes inside" the figure: the women do not know that these figures come apart or understand their internal structure. Men do concede, however, that the women may recognize the legs of the tubuan or dukduk bearer as those of husband or son, though they are not to call the attention of the other women to the identity of the bearer.

Although males themselves feel an aura of mystery and danger about the tubuan, they consciously accentuate this aura when dealing with women and children. Women and children must stay well clear of the tubuan when it appears in the village or they will be fined. Men admonish each other to avoid the tubuan when it is in the sight of women so that the women will think that the men, too, are afraid of it. The Karavarans criticize the men of rival communities for letting their women get too close to the tubuan and for not inculcating proper attitudes of fear and respect in them. The indoctrination of women and children is quite successful. I talked to a very sophisticated adult Tolai, a member of the New Guinea House of Assembly, about his ritual experiences. He said that he had never gone to the taraiu or been to any of the dukduk or tubuan rituals because he had been away at school during the appropriate ages. On one of his visits to the Duke of York Islands in 1968 he unexpectedly came upon a tubuan in the bush and said that he felt the same sharp fear that he had felt as a boy.

During our field work at Karavar, a group of six boys, all in their early teens, saw the tubuan for the first time. This tubuan, which had been made for the funeral of Tonga, a big man, was the first to be made on Karavar for several years. The group was assembled by one of the fathers at a taraiu; each boy carried a fathom of divara and a small basket containing a dish of rice and a tin of corned beef, prestige foods purchased for him by his father and cooked by his mother. After a brief wait the boys were conducted through the woods along the shore until they reached the particular taraiu in which the tubuan was resident. The tubuan was kneeling, surrounded by men seated in a circle. The boys entered this circle, dropped their lengths of divara in front of the kneeling tubuan and sat and nervously ate a few bites of their food. After a few minutes, the tubuan jumped to its feet and the boys fled, only to be caught by the men who still surrounded them. The tubuan danced for a bit, then suddenly removed its uppermost portion, revealing the face of the carrier, a fellow Karavaran. Then the tubuan removed its entire costume, layer by layer, so that the boys could see its construction and the way it was worn. Thus the secrets were revealed to them. The tubuan dressed again and struck the boys on the back with a stick, a form of balilai, after which the senior males, not all of whom were adepts, followed suit. The boys' divara went to the adept who had sponsored the construction of the tubuan.

I was told of two other ways by which the tubuan may reveal its secrets. One is for the novices to surround an unoccupied tubuan and to lift it up unsteadily with sticks. They are told that the tubuan is too dangerous to touch with their hands. As they lift up the mask, it will suddenly overturn and fall to the ground, revealing that it is only a mask rather than a complete indivisible figure. The other way is for the tubuan costume to be occupied by a man who is sitting with his legs hidden. His mask, too, is pried up with sticks but as it is about to overturn, he suddenly jumps to his feet. All three of these methods entail a moment of surprise and fear, followed by the revelation of the secret.

Many of the procedures involved in seeing the tubuan are similar to those followed when a boy first visits the taraiu. In both cases the boys are struck, must pay a small fee of divara or have divara distributed for them, and eat apart from the surrounding circle of initiated males who watch and do not eat. All three—the striking, the payment of a fee, and the eating apart—symbolize the period of transition that precedes full incorporation into the community of males.

The next step in the progression to ritual maturity is to "see the dukduk." This is a minor step and occurs any time that there are dukduks under construction. Dukduks, however, for reasons that will be discussed shortly, are made rather infrequently, generally only every five to ten years. To see the dukduk one merely needs to pay a fathom of divara to the sponsor of the ceremony for which the dukduk is made. If several dukduks are under construction, a youth who has paid this fee once may visit the various construction sites and look at each dukduk as it is made. There is no dramatic unveiling, since it is understood that the tubuan and the dukduk are similar in internal construction and are both

carried by men of the community. Payment to see the dukduk is often just a formality that allows the youth to join one
of the crews making a dukduk.

Buying the Dukduk

Much of the meaning of the dukduk and of the tubuan
stems from a contrast in the way each is purchased and constructed. Purchasing either the dukduk or the tubuan is socially more complex than the earlier ritual stages, and perhaps for this reason is much more expensive. In the stages of
buying the dukduk and the tubuan, the simple opposition between male and female established earlier becomes elaborated
and two kinds of male-to-male relationship are specified.

The purchase of the dukduk is conceptualized as involving
men in balanced relations of reciprocity; the purchase of the
tubuan does not involve men in relations of reciprocity.
When a man buys the dukduk, he ideally gets most of his
divara back along with the dukduk; when a man buys the
tubuan he gets only prestige along with the tubuan. Virtually every male buys the dukduk; very few buy the tubuan. A man who has purchased a dukduk is the ritual equal
of most other men; a man who has purchased the tubuan is
an adept, ritually differentiated from most other men. To
become an adept is to fulfill a major prerequisite in becoming
a big man; it is to move from the essentially noncompetitive
male egalitarianism associated with the dukduk into relationships either of asymmetry as between big man and follower, or of competitive symmetry with other big men, a
symmetry on the order of an arms race. The way in which a
tubuan is purchased puts an emphasis on personal display
and public distributions of divara that is quite lacking in the
purchase of the dukduk but that is in accord with the charac-

teristics of adepts and the context in which the tubuan appears.

One aspect of the reciprocity that characterizes the purchase of the dukduk is revealed in the balancing of past and present ritual performances. The events of purchase of the dukduk are, in particular, related to the events at the time that a boy was first taken to the taraiu.

When a boy first goes to the taraiu, he is usually sponsored by his natal father or stepfather. It often happens, however, that on the day the boy emerges from the taraiu another man will reimburse the father for the divara the father has distributed as his son's sponsor. This payment, referred to as *go kalei*, usually is made by a man who has adopted the boy in question.

When a boy has been adopted, the go kalei of the father by the adoptive father is a statement that the adoptive father wishes to maintain or strengthen a cooperative relationship with the boy's father. If either the father or the adoptive father does not wish such a relationship, then the previous minor ceremony of adoption can be ignored. Karavaran social relations are the expression of current political realities and individual interests rather than of rights exercised or of claims validated. Rights and claims, if they can be said to exist, exist only as an expression of actions that take place for other reasons; they do not have an existence that independently determines action.

If the relationship confirmed through the go kalei between father and adoptive father continues, then the boy will buy the dukduk from his adoptive father. If there was no go kalei, or if the relationship expressed in the go kalei is terminated, then the boy will buy the dukduk from the man who took him to the taraiu, generally his father. The expense of going to the taraiu, and consequently of the go kalei, if there is one, is moderate—around thirty fathoms of divara. The expense of buying a dukduk is substantial—between sixty and one hundred fathoms. Because of this disparity, adoptions are often arranged so that sons are exchanged: each father will go kalei the other and each will then have the other's son buy the dukduk from him.

Such a sequence is not always followed, however. In the vurkurai court, decisions that followed what might be stated in the abstract as normative procedure usually occurred only when the participants were of equal and only moderate importance. Similarly, in the brief ritual biographies that I shall next present, in only one case, that of Toratun, was the norm followed. In the other two cases, those of Alipet and Tilik, the participants were big men and the outcome was not according to abstract norm. Again, I must stress that such an outcome is not regarded by the Karavarans as deviate, as a perversion of the system, or as anything other than the way in which big men often operate.

Case One: Toratun

Toratun was adopted by Alivit and his sister Iamong, who were in Toratun's liting. At that time Iamong was married to Akui. Later Iamong died and Akui remarried. Toratun was taken to the taraiu by his father, Kepas, and by Akui. As a cosponsor Akui was acting as a "father," because he had been married to the woman who, with her brother, had adopted Toratun. Both Akui and Kepas were go kalei-ed by Alivit. Toratun would thus buy the dukduk from Alivit. Alivit had also been active in looking after Toratun's interests and was instrumental in arranging his marriage.

Case Two: Alipet

Alipet has been mentioned as an extremely important man at the height of his power. His father, Bene, and his mother's brother, Tomarmar, were both very big men. Alipet was adopted by a man of little consequence. Bene and Tomarmar demonstrated their power relative to each other and to the adoptive father when Alipet went to the taraiu. Bene and Tomarmar shared the expenses; there was no go kalei. Alipet bought the dukduk from both Bene and Tomarmar with double the usual fee, half going to each. (In this particular case he received only one dukduk, but sometimes under such circumstances two different dukduks are actually purchased and constructed, one from each man.) Alipet was the oldest of his sibling set and he himself took his younger brother, Mitiate, to the taraiu. As Mitiate was not adopted, Alipet took the place of their father, Bene. Bene, who was still alive at this time, in effect stepped aside so that Alipet could have his brother buy a dukduk from him. This gesture is some-times made by a father, especially if he is a very big man, in the pervasive belief that such a transaction should be an exchange—that the divara from purchase of the dukduk should return in some way. This actually means, however, that the eldest son of a big man is given an appreciable finan-cial boost by his father. If a boy buys a dukduk when he is still a youth and a dependent, he will never pay back the divara given to him for his purchase. If the boy buys from his father, the father will often privately advance him the divara only to receive it back publicly. Thus Alipet expended none of his own divara as a boy to purchase a dukduk, yet as an adult he was able to keep the fee given to him for his brother Mitiate.

Case Three: Tilik

Tilik, like Alipet, was the son and sister's son of very important men. He was taken to the taraiu by his father, Kaliop, and by his mother's brother, Toapek. Although Tilik had been adopted, there was no go kalei. Later Tilik purchased a dukduk from both Kaliop and Toapek with separate fees going to each. His father, Kaliop, received the larger amount of one hundred fathoms; Toapek received sixty fathoms. Each had a dukduk constructed for Tilik, although the dukduks were identical and both carried the same name. Later, Kaliop go kalei-ed the father of Kaliop's own adopted son when this boy went to the taraiu. He then had this boy purchase the dukduk from Tilik. The divara for Tilik's own purchase of a dukduk from Kaliop and Toapek had come from Toapek, Kaliop, and Tilik's mother, not from Tilik himself. But the fee paid to Tilik by the boy Kaliop had adopted—all eighty fathoms—was kept by Tilik and was largely profit.

In each of these cases, the boy's father had an important part, in accordance with the often stated view that a father should escort his son through the early ritual stages. The difference between cases concerned the role that an adoptive father was allowed to play. Toratun's case was made complex because there were in effect two adoptive fathers, one of whom bought out the other one. Kepas displayed great scrupulousness in allowing Akui to assist him in taking Toratun to the taraiu; Alivit behaved with similar scrupulousness by including Akui in the go kalei. No one of these participants was an important man and no one was powerful enough to eclipse the others. Consequently even Akui's highly tenuous interests in Toratun were recognized.

In the cases of Alipet and Tilik, the adoptive father also was an unimportant individual, but his interests could be ignored because the father and mother's brother were big men. If the father had been less powerful, then the adoptive father would have go kalei-ed him; if the mother's brother had been less powerful, he would not have featured at all. In both cases, the importance of mother's brother and father is unambiguously demonstrated by the way they cooperated with one another and ignored the interests of the adoptive father—who probably would not even make an effort to assert his interests.

Although Tilik's father, Kaliop, did not acknowledge Tilik's adoptive father's interests in Tilik, nonetheless Kaliop was able to assert his own interests as an adoptive father in another man's son. Such behavior is typical of the way a big man is able to redefine reciprocal transactions to his own advantage. In cases concerning adoption this is done usually by asserting that the adoptive father has not acted as an adoptive father: he has not given his adopted son the consistent support and the various gifts of clothing and food that constitute the relationship. Of course, no one would be likely to call into question a big man's behavior toward his own adopted children.

Thus, where the father is so important that he is unwilling to share his interests in his son, he may ignore the interests of lesser men, who in turn are reluctant to assert them. Conversely, where the father is of sufficient unimportance, an adoptive father sometimes does not bother to assert his interests in his adopted son. Such was the case of Topalangut, Topap's father. I did not mention in my earlier account that Topap had been adopted by a man on the neighboring island of Utuan and that Topalangut notified him at the time

Topap was to go to the taraiu. However, for reasons that were not entirely clear—or that no one wanted to talk about—the adoptive father did not come forth and hence did not go kalei Topalangut. Thus when I asked Topalangut at the time whether anyone had adopted Topap, he said "No!" I did not get the other side of the story, but I suspect that Topalangut's unexceptional status, plus the relatively short notice of the whole affair, more than offset the possible advantages of gaining ritual control over Topap. The other party then simply dropped this opportunity to maintain and strengthen a social tie with Topalangut through his son.

The ritual events of a boy going to the taraiu and of buying a dukduk are viewed as situations in which males enter into reciprocal relations with each other, as adults or as father and son. As in all aspects of Karavaran life, big men usually define the situation to their own advantage, whereas lesser men are more circumspect in asserting themselves. When big men participate in these ritual events, however, they still maneuver within the framework of the model of reciprocal relationships as concerns adopting a child, taking a boy to the taraiu, go kalei-ing, and buying the dukduk. A big man will still follow this pattern although he may in effect deny that his son was adopted. If he does deny the adoption he can ignore the interests of an adoptive father so that there is no go kalei when the big man's son goes to the taraiu. And because there was no go kalei, the big man can have his son buy the dukduk from him. He might, as in Alipet's and Tilik's case, carry the pattern of reciprocity even further by transferring his ritual interests in another boy to his own son. Such a transfer goes beyond even the usual generosity of father to son.

In such ways, even when the principals are big men, the

forms of reciprocity—and with them the implicit premise of male equality—are preserved in these ritual transactions. There remains a consistent association of going to the taraiu and buying the dukduk from the "father"—either natal, step, or adoptive father: there is a consistent association of the dukduk with the kinds of transactions of reciprocity and equality that are represented by the father-son relationship.

The formally noncompetitive relationships associated with the dukduk derive much of their meaning from an implicit juxtaposition with the formally competitive relationships associated with the tubuan. The significance of the actual construction of the dukduk, which is part of its purchase, derives much of its meaning from an explicit juxtaposition with the actual construction of the tubuan. The Karavarans consciously define each figure through juxtaposition with the other and the very circumstances in which each is made suggest such a comparison.

The only occasion at which a dukduk can be constructed—and hence purchased—is at a *matamatam*. This is the most important of the Duke of York rituals: it is a mortuary ceremony defined by the presence of both dukduks and tubuans. The dukduk can be made only in conjunction with a tubuan, although a tubuan can appear alone or with just other tubuans. As a consequence, the purchase of the dukduk can be fully understood only as the significance of the tubuan is understood. That is to say, the dukduk can be understood only in the context of the matamatam.

A matamatam requires the greatest expenditure of cash, divara and communal effort of any Karavaran activity. At least one man—either an aspiring or an established big man—must act as a sponsor. His decision to sponsor a matamatam rests on a variety of considerations: his supply of cash and divara; his appraisal of his future commitments; his control over a following; his ritual debts to other big men which can be paid off only during a matamatam. Another major consideration which affects the frequency and timing of a matamatam is the configuration at a particular time of intra- and intercommunity political relationships. An individual will sponsor a matamatam so that he will be recognized or confirmed as a big man. The more that political relationships are in flux, the more likely that there will be men who wish to assert themselves against their rivals by sponsoring a matamatam. Conversely, the more that the existing political relationships are static, the less likely that men will sponsor a matamatam. As a consequence, matamatams are staged at quite uneven intervals. The most recent on Karavara at the time of our 1968 field work had been in the late 1950's. During 1968 the Karavarans were just making the necessary preliminary preparations for one, which was held in 1969, after our departure. Another matamatam was held during 1972.

In addition, there are two major considerations of a communal rather than of an individual nature. One of these concerns the explicit purpose of the mortuary ceremony which is to "finish" (rap) those of a particular moiety who have died since the last matamatam. If there has been a long period—ten years between matamatams is a long period—then many individuals will have close relatives whom they want to "finish" as part of a matamatam sponsored by a big man. This is one source of community pressure. Another kind of pressure and one germane to my consideration of the ritual of buying the dukduk is that the male community may feel that there are too many young men who have not yet bought the dukduk.

An individual who has not yet bought the dukduk is in the eyes of Karavarans not yet fully a male. Not that he is a potential source of contamination to other men as, for instance, the uncircumcised Ndembu youth is to the ritually mature men (Turner 1967); rather, he is limited—or should be limited—in his relations with women. This limitation obtains in both a ritual and a nonritual context.

Until he has purchased a dukduk, a youth is not allowed to carry a tubuan, considered to be female, nor can he enter the house where the vanai has been hidden on the occasion when a boy is abducted from the village to be taken to the taraiu. (When Topap went to the taraiu, both of the young men who carried him off were fined by the kilung court because they had not yet bought the dukduk.) Both of these restrictions indicate that a youth must limit his contact with females until he himself is ritually differentiated from them and hence fully a male.

Furthermore, a man is not supposed to marry until he has bought a dukduk. The Karavarans see a clear parallel between buying a dukduk and getting married; the purchase of the male dukduk should precede the purchase of a woman. This priority is frequently expressed in spatial terms: "a man should marry [buy the dukduk] first on the beach [on the men's ground] and then later in the village [the women's province]." The parallels between the two kinds of "marriage" are thought in part to lie in the way the divara for the dukduk and for the bride are collected and transferred. At the time of our study, there were a number of young Karavaran men who were married and had fathered children but who had not purchased the dukduk. The older men often talked about this and felt that it was an unfortunate state of affairs that should be corrected. The presence of such young men who are behaving as socially adult although they are not yet ritually adult is another kind of pressure leading to the performance of a matamatam.

A matamatam has a rather standard series of preliminary activities which may last a year or longer. It is only during the final several weeks that the dukduks and tubuans are constructed at the taraiu. When the dukduks and tubuans are made the men stay almost exclusively at the taraiu. During this period of seclusion, called a *kumbak*, contact of any sort with women is strictly enjoined and male solidarity is at its highest: the men gloat to each other that theirs is an important activity from which women are excluded, and they reminisce about kumbaks of the past.

The activity of the kumbak provides the core of meaning to the purchase of the dukduk—and hence to the meaning of the figure itself. It defines a community of males who demonstrate their completeness by creating—in the absence of women—another male, the dukduk. In no other context is the contrast between male and female so sharply drawn and in no other context is the essentially noncompetitive, reciprocal father-son kind of interaction so nearly the exclusive model of male-to-male interaction.

At the time of the kumbak when a young man buys the dukduk, the particular one that he is purchasing should in theory be constructed for him; however, I was told that if there are many novices buying dukduks the available work force or funds may not be sufficient for a dukduk to be made for each of them. Thus there may be big plans for having twenty dukduks appear for twenty men who are buying them, but these plans are generally not carried out. Instead a group of brothers or half brothers, men who share either a father or mother—and these may be understood in a fairly extended sense, will have only one dukduk actually made for them. The men who are thus grouped together may in fact all be purchasing different dukduk patterns and those whose dukduks are not actually being made may just be shown drawings of them.

The work force for each dukduk tends to be composed of both matrilineal and patrilateral kin. If a boy is buying the dukduk from his father, the construction group may include his father, his father's brother, his father's sons, and his father's sister's sons. Such a work group may also include an adept because some of the spells acquired with the purchase of the tubuan are necessary for dukduk construction. Adopted sons are another class of helpers. Generally only a big man can count on these as consistent followers in any situation in which their close kinsmen could use their services. In addition, since all males in the community assist in one or more of these work groups, strays are included under the aegis of extended kinship links. For instance, any senior man of the opposite moiety could be included as a "father."

After the work on the dukduks has been completed, the kumbak is concluded and males can come and go freely between the village and the taraiu. The public part of the matamatam begins: now both dukduks and tubuans appear frequently in the village; on prearranged days large numbers of men and women from other communities visit and are given divara; big men strut about dispensing and receiving aggressive hospitality. At this point in the matamatam, the dukduks no longer hold the dominant attention that they did in the kumbak; they are secondary in overall importance to the tubuan. Correspondingly, the pattern of male solidarity gives way to overt competition between big men, based on ownership of divara and control of followers. Nonetheless, even though the dukduk and its associated pattern of non-competitive interaction may be eclipsed, it is by no means ignored.

On the day the dukduks and tubuans leave the taraiu to go into the village, each figure is ceremonially struck with divara, usually ten fathoms, provided by the man who has sponsored the figure's construction. If the sponsor is an adept, he will strike his own dukduk. If not, he must make arrangements for an adept to strike, using the sponsor's divara. There is no fee for this service.

During the next few days all the dukduks and tubuans go from the taraiu into the village to dance. Then all the dukduks and tubuans go individually from the taraiu into the village where they receive gifts of betel nut and divara. The term for this is *wamama*, which means to present betel nut, a common sign of courtesy. Each dukduk, my informants told me, will go to the hamlet of the parents of the boy who is purchasing it. As it kneels on the ground, first men and then women approach it and throw down packages of betel nuts and peppers along with short lengths of divara which all belong to the boy who is buying the dukduk.

During our 1968 stay in the field, no one on Karavar bought a dukduk. A dukduk that had been made on a neighboring island, however, visited Karavar to receive such a presentation of betel nut and divara. The following account of that visit illustrates the way in which the men's society of the dukduk and tubuan establishes links between different island communities. It also demonstrates a kind of cooperation that is completely absent at the time the tubuan is purchased.

I had heard on Karavar that the men on Mualim, another island in the Duke of York group, had been kumbaking and that a number were purchasing dukduks. Two people from Karavar, Nemeya and Kongkong, were in attendance there. Nemeya had been born on Karavar but had lived uxorilocally for many years on Mualim, a slightly unusual circumstance since most marriages are within the community or with its closest neighboring ally, which in the Karavaran case is Utuan. After his wife's death Nemeya had returned to Karavar. By this wife he had two sons, Tolaplapir and Tokanamur. Both had grown up and married on Mualim, but they occasionally visited Karavar, especially after their father moved back there. These two were purchasing a dukduk from Nemeya. All three of them would share the ownership of this single dukduk—an arrangement not uncommon for dukduks but quite uncommon for tubuans. Kongkong, a Karavaran, had been asked by Nemeya to help in the construction of this dukduk. As an adept, he knew the spells for construction of the dukduk, and he was familiar with the design of the particular dukduk under construction. Furthermore, he was a skilled workman. Although Kongkong was the expert of his work crew, he was paid only slightly more than the worker's standard fee of one fathom of divara. Since men enjoy the kumbak, however, I suspect that Kongkong was happy to participate.

The Karavarans knew that this kumbak was going on at Mualim; nevertheless, they were surprised one morning when a small work boat owned by a man from Mualim arrived with the dukduk in full regalia. The boat landed at the taraiu and Nemeya, his two sons, Kongkong, and several Mualims disembarked along with the dukduk itself. The dukduk had come to collect gifts of betel nut and divara in reciprocation for an earlier visit made by some Karavarans to Mualim.

Some years before, in the late 1950's, Tiloi had bought a dukduk on Karavar. He had then gone with his dukduk to Mualim to seek gifts. His entree there was through his true mother's brother, Nemeya. Two other Karavarans, Teventui and Taki, who also had just purchased dukduks, tagged along with Tiloi. Nemeya's wife presented divara to Tiloi's dukduk in the name of her then small sons, Tolaplapir and Tokanamur, the same two who were now buying a dukduk. Their dukduk was now coming to Karavar to collect the repayment of this earlier debt since Tiloi was obligated to repay Nemeya's wife's donation to his dukduk by giving an identical amount to the sons in whose name it had been given.

After the dukduk had arrived on Karavar it periodically ventured out from the taraiu into the village, scattering women and children, who are forbidden under normal circumstances to approach either a tubuan or dukduk. Around 3:30 P.M. preparations for a small feast began at the taraiu. Tiloi was primarily in charge of these preparations assisted by Teventui and Taki. The meager amount of food soon provoked murmured comments that the preparations for the meal had been inadequate. Furthermore, there was no taro. To the non-Karavaran this may sound like a reprieve rather than a disaster, but taro is considered to be the essential item at any important feast.

The seating arrangement at the taraiu for this meal was significant: Nemeya was given a prestigious position next to Alipet, the most important of the adepts, and was the first to be served. Nemeya was accorded these signs of respect, more than he usually received, because it was his dukduk that was present. The Mualim visitors were served next because they were guests, and then the Karavarans. Tiloi, the main pro-

vider of the food, ate last to make sure there was enough to
go around. It was apparent that there really was not enough.
(Later that night there was a special meeting of the kilung
court called by Alipet as the senior adept. Tiloi, Teventui,
and Taki were asked to explain why their preparations had
been so meager and why there had been no publicity so that
other men as well could have helped. The three men successfully defended themselves by saying they thought the dukduk would collect gifts and then return to Mualim immediately without there being a feast. The court accepted this
explanation. This was the only case I knew of in which a
mistake in ritual brought to the kilung court did not result in
a fine.)

After the meal the men drifted into the village to Tiloi's
trade store where the dukduk would be given the gifts for
Nemeya's two sons. After a short time the dukduk itself arrived from the taraiu, knelt on the ground in front of the
store, and received the gift packets of betel nut and divara.
As usual, men approached the dukduk first, then the women.
Most of the packets carried tags naming those for whom they
were being given. These named contributions were either to
repay a similar gift received in the past or were to open new
debts. Tiloi paid back the two fathoms of divara to Nemeya's
sons that had been given to his dukduk in their name by their
mother about ten years earlier. Tiloi's wife also gave a
fathom in the name of their oldest son, who had yet to purchase a dukduk. Thus the relationship of debt was renewed.

Several young men who had not yet bought the dukduk
but were old enough to control their own divara gave in their
own names. Only one man gave in the name of his sister's
son. This was Koniel whose socially precarious position has
already been discussed with respect to a case in the vurkurai

court. Koniel was unmarried and had no sons for whom he could give; however, he did have one genealogically very close sister's son. Most of Koniel's efforts to enlarge his kin group on Karavar had been unsuccessful. Perhaps as a consequence he was especially concerned with strengthening his hold on those few kinsmen he already had. He took this occasion to behave in exemplary fashion to a sister's son. His generosity was all the more striking for occurring at a time when most men limit their generosity to their own sons.

Following the presentations the dukduk returned to the taraiu and the visitors departed for Mualim. It was estimated that thirty fathoms of divara had been collected. The divara belonged to Nemeya's sons to be spent by them as they pleased, although there was the expectation that it would cover some of the expenses of buying the dukduk. Adult men, such as Nemeya's sons, are more likely to pay at least part of their own way than are those who are only boys or adolescents at the time of their purchase. The debts that were paid back to them were profit, since this divara had originally been given in their names by other people. The debts that were initiated at the time of this visit were the responsibility of Nemeya's sons to repay, and by accepting these new debts they committed themselves to future participation in their father's community. There is probably no way that they could have collected the old debts without acquiring, on the same occasion, new ones.

An important contrast between the dukduk and tubuan lies in the nature of these presentations. The tubuan, too, is given betel nut and divara but the enduring reciprocal relations of debt are not established; the contributions to the tubuan are not paid back and hence are not marked with an individual's name.

The next step in the purchase of the dukduk is to assemble the *tagan* in the village.[4] The tagan is a small decorated basket containing an assortment of cigarettes, pieces of tobacco, firecrackers, waistcloths, plates, spoons, and short lengths of divara. In addition, there may be several large flat sea shells called *kalang*, which also figure in a marriage presentation. These modest items are contributed by members of the young man's liting as well as by his father.

The tagan is woven by the young man's mother and is similar in design to a woman's carrying basket. It is explicitly compared to the small basket the bride's mother weaves for her daughter's marriage ceremony. The tagan—both basket and contents—remains in the village with the young man's mother until the day when the divara is actually transferred for the purchase of the dukduk.

The reason usually given for the purchase of a dukduk before a young man is married is that it would be a matter of great shame for his tagan to stay with his wife rather than with his mother. This rationale suggests that before a young man buys a dukduk his association with women should be of a nonsexual nature: he should associate with a mother rather than with a wife. It is consistent with the Karavaran view that the purchase of the dukduk is itself a kind of marriage that should precede the marriage with a female—a kind of union between males, an expression of male solidarity. The dukduk is a male figure constructed only by males, under conditions of complete seclusion from females. The only females who should be at all involved are the sexually prohibited women of the liting, most specifically the young man's mother. A mother, in contrast to a wife, is relatively un-

---

[4] I did not personally witness the collection of the tagan nor the subsequent transfer of divara for the purchase of the dukduk.

polluting to a man and is, moreover, much more closely associated with his permanent interests, such as his purchase of the dukduk or tubuan.

On the last day of the matamatam, the tagan, together with the sixty to one hundred fathoms that constitute the bulk of the purchase price, is presented to the man from whom the dukduk is purchased. If the young man is purchasing from his father, an older brother or sometimes a mother's brother will present the tagan and divara to the father. If he is purchasing from someone other than his father, such as from an adoptive father, his father will make the presentation.

The recipient of this presentation will calculate the value in divara of the European goods in the tagan that were purchased with money. The rate of exchange used is the orthodox one which makes two shillings (A$.20) the equivalent of one fathom of divara. In actuality this conversion rate tends to inflate the total of divara, since a more realistic exchange rate, based on the cash value of trade goods which are then sold for divara, would be seven or eight shillings to one fathom. The value of the tagan reckoned in divara is then added to the rest of the divara presented and the recipient announces the total to the men assembled at the taraiu.

In exchange for this purchase fee, the young man receives the right to sponsor the construction of any dukduk as well as the copyright to a particular pattern of dukduk. He also gets a quantity of food called a *palom*, provided by the man from whom the dukduk is purchased and including prepared indigenous foods as well as such European foods as rice and tinned meat, and other items such as tobacco. The young man will eat the prepared indigenous foods, but he can sell the other items in the village for divara. In theory, at least, he is able to recoup the expenses of purchasing a dukduk by reselling the palom. But in practice I strongly doubt that these goods are ever sufficient in quantity for him to get back in this way more than a small fraction of the total purchase price. Also, during such a resale, to judge by a similar kind of conversion that takes place during a wedding, very substandard payments in divara may be given.

Virtually every male passes through the sequence of ritual grades that culminates with the purchase of the dukduk. As he progresses, his maleness is developed and with the purchase of the dukduk he is fully incorporated into the community of males. Consistent with the development of common maleness are the egalitarian relationships established through a pattern of pervasive reciprocity. The mutual adoption of sons, the boy's first visit to the taraiu, the go kalei, the purchase of the dukduk—all are seen as composing a sequence of reciprocal relations. Even the purchase of the dukduk is seen not as the end of this sequence but rather as a step to other reciprocal transactions. Karavarans say that the divara spent on a dukduk is not lost, for it can return in several possible ways: through resale of the palom; through a younger sibling buying from a brother who has in turn bought from his father; and through the seller of the dukduk acting as the marriage sponsor for the man who bought the dukduk from him.

The Purchase of the Tubuan

Men buy the tubuan not in order to be the ritual equal of other men but to be their ritual superior: they become adepts in the hope that they will become big men, although many adepts never do in fact become big men. The reciprocity entailed in the prior ritual grades is lacking in the purchase of the tubuan. There is no concept that the divara spent on the tubuan will return, there are no relations of reciprocal debt established to raise the purchase price of the tubuan. The social relations that form the context of the tubuan are competitive rather than cooperative.

A tubuan, unlike a dukduk, can be made and purchased any time there is a class of sufficient size to make the undertaking worthwhile for the teacher.[5] Men in a given area who are interested in buying the tubuan are generally known to each other; the more important of these will approach a suitable teacher.

The first consideration in the choice of a teacher is his moiety. A man ordinarily buys the tubuan from a senior member of his own moiety—a classificatory mother's brother. One reason is that the individually named tubuans are themselves associated with a particular moiety: there are Pikalambe tubuans and Maramar tubuans. The individual tubuans an adept can give to the members of his class as their own are largely restricted to the tubuans of his own moiety. Consistent with the symbolic association of the tubuan with affairs within the moiety—to be explored later—men prefer to buy a tubuan of their own moiety. Only if a man's father is asked to be a teacher will a man normally buy a tubuan from a member of the opposite moiety. A son may join such a class, although the other members are likely to be of the same moiety as their teacher.

Relations within the moiety are characterized by competition and feelings of ambivalence. Because the teacher and the class are of the same moiety, special care must be taken in selecting a particular adept as teacher. A man who buys the tubuan is able, assuming other necessary characteristics, to become a big man and thus to become a possible rival to the

[5] The last class on Karavar was in the late 1950's.

established big man. It would be a mistake, therefore, to ask an adept to take a class if he felt his position was threatened. He might, by refusing to accept the class, humiliate those who had approached him; he might even attack with sorcery these men who were thus showing themselves as potential rivals; or, worst of all, he might accept the class but intentionally teach incorrect or incomplete spells which would not protect a man against the power of the tubuan.

I mentioned earlier that Karavarans often say that a man should use the spells that his father taught him rather than those spells comprising part of the formal purchase of the tubuan. I have no doubt that Karavarans would feel safer using their father's spells than the spells taught them by a mother's brother. However, because few men are adepts, most men do not have adepts as fathers. Moreover, a man's father is often dead by the time he becomes old enough to consider buying a tubuan. For these reasons ,it is clear that most of the men who buy the tubuan plan to use spells that are part of the purchase.

As a consequence, they desire to find a teacher who is trustworthy and has a reputation for knowing high quality spells. He should be a man enjoying good health—that is, a man whose spells have given him full protection from the tubuan. His mortuary ceremonies should be spectacular, exciting the envy of visitors. A dilemma arises here, however, since a man who gives very successful ceremonies clearly has such effective magic that he might be something of a sorcerer, and hence not trustworthy. Tonga was such a man. Many men wanted to learn his superior magic but they were afraid he would teach them the incorrect spells or would sorcerize them.

During our study there was a class of Pikalambe men on

Karavar ready to purchase the tubuan from Alipet, also a Pikalambe. Three other Karavaran Pikalambe men at this same time instead joined another class and bought the tubuan at Mioko from a mother's brother named Tomas. Their defection caused a stir on Karavar, especially because Karavar and Mioko are traditional rivals. Moreover, these three Karavarans were regarded by the Karavaran big men as impatient upstarts. Ironically, as it turned out, the Karavaran class grew impatient with Alipet's delays and finally, in 1970, it too made its purchase from Tomas of Mioko. The following account is of the 1968 purchase at Mioko by the three Karavarans and their class.

When I arrived at Mioko in the morning I was told that the class had spent their first night drinking at the taraiu there. Some, at least, had expected that Tomas would tell them the ritual secrets necessary for the construction of the tubuan that night and were disappointed that he just reiterated what is common knowledge among men: the tubuan should be made for sufficient cause. The significance of this advice rests in the association of the tubuan with big men. The magnitude of the ceremony for which the tubuan is constructed constitutes one of the tests of whether a tubuan's sponsor is a big man. A meager ceremony or no ceremony at all would not constitute sufficient cause for its construction: the symbolic link which defines the man who constructs a tubuan as a big man would be broken. If a tubuan is made for insufficient cause, then its spirit will not return to its home in the sunset at the conclusion of the ceremony but will linger and afflict the errant adept with a wasting and fatal illness. The matamatam is a series of such tests whereby the man who makes the tubuan must prove that he is a big man.

The following morning the Mioko class went through the public part of their purchase of the tubuan called the *kavei*. A striking feature of the kavei is that at this time alone women can behave with relative familiarity toward the tubuan. Furthermore, women as a category are given divara by the class. Women of the surrounding communities flocked to Mioko, drawn by these two prospects.

According to myth, a woman was the original owner of the tubuan. The spirit of the tubuan, a *turangan*, first appeared to a woman while she was gardening. It taught her the spells and techniques for the construction of the tubuan. Later she made a tubuan but her hushand and the other men took it from her, and since then matters relating to the tubuan have been secrets kept by the men from the women. At the time of the kavei when a new group of men purchases the tubuan, women's original association with it is explicitly acknowledged.

At the Mioko kavei, women arrived *en masse* from Karavar, Utuan and other neighboring communities. Each community group marched along the village path from the beaches into Tomas's hamlet. As they entered the hamlet, the class, accompanied by Tomas's tubuan, charged out at them. During this encounter, when the women were physically very close to the tubuan, they performed a kind of arrogant dance step called *malamala* and waved spears. All of these activities are usually prohibited to women and the dancing and spear waving are usually restricted to the adepts alone.

After the several processions of women had been greeted at Tomas's hamlet in this way, the distribution of divara began. The members of the class, led by Tomas, filed in front of a long row of seated adepts from Karavar, Utuan, and Mioko. Each adept was given divara by each member of the class. Next, the class gave divara to the women in general. In the latter distribution they were helped by a few of their close female matrilineal kin: their mothers, sisters, and mother's sisters. Some of these women, especially a novice's mother, may have helped him prior to the kavei with an outright gift of divara; all of them helped their kinsman at the kavei by following after him, supplementing his distribution of divara to the women with their own.

In the kavei, women are differentiated into those who received divara and those close matrilineal kin who assisted a member of the class. The women of the liting who do help in the kavei are called "women of the tubuan" (*vavina na tubuan*). They are entitled to certain limited privileges denied to other women with respect to the particular tubuan that they have helped purchase. Only these women are permitted to call out the name of this tubuan and to perform the malamala dance on any occasion when it is made.

The association of these women of the liting with the tubuan is appropriate since both women and tubuans are associated with matrilineal continuity. Not only is a particular tubuan associated with a moiety, it is also likely to be associated with a particular liting in that moiety. In fact, it may bear the name of a woman thought to be a liting ancestress. In some cases, a newly created tubuan is named after its owner's mother.

The kavei concluded with a large feast at the Mioko taraiu provided by Tomas for all of the men present on Mioko. After the meal a number of men spoke of how impressive the proceedings had been; others wondered whether the women had been pleased with the kavei. With these speeches the kavei ended, although the class members were not yet fully accredited adepts. They had not been taught the spells or the ritual to use in constructing and controlling the tubuan, nor had each been given exclusive rights to a particular tubuan. This all was to come later in the *waturpat*.

The waturpat for this group did not take place during our 1968 study. I did, however, piece together from various accounts of past waturpat ceremonies an overall picture of the events. The waturpat is a ceremony requiring the same expenses and procedure as a mortuary ceremony except that in the waturpat no mortuary responsibilities are discharged. The expenditures of the waturpat are all the more impressive for lacking a "practical" goal.

During the waturpat the teacher gives each member of the class a particular named tubuan, called the *kambina* (base, root) tubuan, which is to be his exclusive property while he lives. The kambina tubuan is usually drawn from the ample stock of existing but currently unallocated tubuans associated with a particular moiety and often with a liting of that moiety. These tubuans, as I have indicated, are property over which the teacher as a big man in his moiety exercises some control. A man's kambina tubuan should belong to his own moiety. If the novice is of the same moiety as his teacher, there is no problem. However, if he purchases a tubuan from his father or from some other member of his father's moiety, adjustments can be made.

It can, for instance, be asserted by the new adept that his kambina tubuan is associated with his own moiety simply because it is his kambina tubuan, irrespective of the tubuan's earlier moiety affiliations. A slightly more imaginative tack is for a man to say that his tubuan has always been associated with his moiety but was just out on loan for a period to the members of the opposite moiety. It is the association of the kambina tubuan with the matrilineal group, not the way this association may be justified, that is important.

The waturpat consists largely in the construction and display of the kambina tubuans under the supervision of the teacher. At this time he teaches the spells necessary for the construction of the tubuan and the conduct of a mortuary ceremony. The expenses of the waturpat are shared by students and the teacher. In Tomas's case, his expenses would be particularly heavy because he would organize and attend waturpats on Karavar, Utuan, and Mioko for the class members of these communities. Although a teacher is believed to make a profit from the fees he receives from his class, it is unlikely that this is often the case. However, just as the waturpat when performed in a particularly lavish fashion can catapult a new adept into the front rank of the adepts, so also substantial expenses borne by the teacher can similarly enhance his prestige.

Extravagance in ritual performances is one of the bases of prestige. The kavei and the waturpat place both the teacher and student in the spotlight so that their distribution of divara can render them maximum prestige. There will of course be appreciable differences between individuals in the extent to which each is able to take advantage of such opportunities. As a consequence there are both important and unimportant adepts.

Extravagance is most effective if it is done with style. Tomerau, an important Karavaran, told me of the waturpat some years before when Alipet and two others, now dead, put on a fine performance. He said admiringly that although they probably spent one hundred fathoms of divara they did it as though they were laughing. Nonchalance in expending divara is the mark of a really big man.

Much of the meaning of the tubuan is implicit in the context in which it is purchased. It is consistently associated with relations within the matrimoiety: A tubuan is usually purchased from a mother's brother—a big man of the moiety—in order to establish or consolidate power within the moiety. The particular named tubuan figures are considered the property of the moiety, and are often associated with a particular liting. The name of a man's tubuan is often that of a woman of his own liting. A man is helped in his purchase of the tubuan by women of his liting. A tubuan is constructed during a mortuary ceremony to finish the dead of a particular moiety. Moreover, the tubuan has an undying spirit which suggests an association with the permanence of the matrimoieties.

The association of the tubuan with intramoiety relations, especially as these relations concern the control by big men of their followers with divara, receives additional support and amplification when the qualities of the tubuan spirit are examined. The spirit of the tubuan is not only enduring; it is also powerful, difficult to control, and potentially very dangerous; it is vital and disruptive. As such, I suggest, it is an image of the vital and disruptive qualities of man's momboto nature on which are based the competitive, coercive relationships within the moiety. Perhaps also the enduring nature of this dangerous spirit is a statement that momboto nature itself is unchanging.

A defining feature of a big man is his ritual capacity to bring the tubuan under control: a big man is able to domesticate its wild spirit just as he is able to constrain his followers through the use of divara. The major purpose of a matamatam is to bring the tubuan and the big man into conjunction, providing a test of a big man's power to impose order on others as shown through his control of the tubuan. But the tubuan also constrains the big man: it limits his power and imposes an order on him as well.

Although I have at this point given only a preliminary discussion of the meaning of the tubuan, this material should help the reader understand the events of the kavei, centered as they are on the tubuan and the adept.

If tubuans are associated with big men, they are also associated with women. The events of the kavei make a statement, not only about big men and power, but also about the relations between men and women. Women are regarded as the original owners of the tubuan; women, as a category, are presented divara along with adepts at the kavei; particular women help their sons buy a tubuan and are referred to thereafter as "women of the tubuan"; during the final speeches at the taraiu men wonder if the women were pleased with the kavei.

The question arises: why is it believed that women once owned the tubuan? Or, to rephrase the question, what do women and adepts have in common? In most respects, they have little in common. Adepts have power that they use to impose order; women have no power and often subvert order. Men are active agents who regard woman as elusive and desirable objects. Yet the implication is clear that because women at one time did control the tubuan, they too acted for a limited time as adepts. With the kavei, they are again acting like adepts. I suggest that the kavei is a statement to women that they are still, as they were at one time, capable of upholding rather than subverting order. Moreover, the kavei shows that certain women—that is, "women of the tubuan"—are more like the adepts than other women. Through their support of the novices who are buying the tubuan these particular women of the liting demonstrate their acceptance of the male perspective which holds that the big man/adept provides the basis of society. Inasmuch as a "woman of the tubuan" shares the perspective of her son—the new adept—she is allowed to interact on other occasions with the tubuan in a way similar to that of an adept.

The "women of the tubuan" have committed themselves during the kavei to upholding social order. As "mothers," they have accepted the constraints of divara and moiety in bride price and marriage; as "mothers," their sexuality is focused on reproduction, which strengthens rather than divides society; as "mothers," they accept the male perspective by supporting their sons in becoming adepts; as supporters of their sons they are supporting with divara the principle that social order is based on divara. In all of this they contrast with the other image of women: women of the opposite moiety who are sexually desirable and physically polluting; women who run off to other men and let their fathers and husbands fight over the bride price.

The kavei is in part, I suggest, an effort to make women controllable: to induce them, by accepting divara, to allow themselves to be ordered by it. By thus accepting divara as the standard of order they would support social order as they once did when they controlled the tubuan and acted as adepts. Most important, during the kavei, the "women of the tubuan" are singled out to be models and agents of domestication for other women.

"Were the women pleased by the kavei?" the men asked themselves. If the kavei is, as I have suggested, the effort by men to domesticate the women as they had once been at the time when they controlled the tubuan, then perhaps this question asked if the effort was successful. Clearly some women had responded to this domestication—the "women of the tubuan"—but what of the others? The men have doubts.

A final question concerns the reason for this focus on

women at the time that a new group of men are becoming adepts. An adept is one who controls society. This control is both symbolized and made possible by his control of the tubuan. At the time that a man is becoming an adept, he is taught what the nature of the society is that an adept controls. One critical event in the kavei is the presentation of divara by the class to the current adepts as well as to all of the women. Women and adepts are thus lumped together and, in a sense, together represent society. Both are necessary for its continuity: its social and physical continuity if women can be induced to accept the constraints of divara and be induced to act as "mothers"; its social continuity if adepts can be induced to accept divara with its constraints as the sole medium of their power. Perhaps too this same view that women and adepts together represent society is shown in the figure of the tubuan. The tubuan is female. It also is that image of power-divara-domestication that is embodied in the big man/adept. An understanding of the relationship of women and adepts is in part an understanding of the meaning of the figure of the tubuan that the class is purchasing. If women and adepts together are equivalent to the tubuan, controlling them with divara replicates the control of the tubuan with divara during the mortuary ceremony.

CHAPTER 5

Preliminary Stages in the Mortuary Cycle

The most general term for a mortuary ceremony, which is distinct from a funeral, is *balanguan*. Balanguans may or may not have tubuans or dukduks. In fact, a liu, mentioned earlier, is a balanguan in which there are no tubuans, and hence no dukduks, and for that reason a liu is usually given by men who are not adepts. My major concern, however, will be the analysis of a matamatam, a balanguan defined by the presence of both dukduks and tubuans.

A mortuary ceremony has the explicit purpose of finishing the dead.[1] When the dead are finished, the Karavarans say, the living no longer have to think of them. The dead that are of most importance in a balanguan are usually deceased big men. A big man gives existence to an apik; consequently, his followers are adrift after his death. Only when these followers are incorporated into an apik focused on another big man can their former big man be forgotten; only then is he finished. Finishing the dead involves the replacement of one big man by another big man. A balanguan, then, concerns succession and continuity, matters of particular importance to the Karavarans because they lack a concept of office.

Since to be a big man means to act as a big man—to enter

[1] Although the dead can be contacted during fasts in the deep forest by men seeking songs and magic, they are neither aware of nor concerned with whether a mortuary ceremony has been made for them.

into relations with followers, to control the tubuan, and so on,—the crucial question, as I have earlier suggested, becomes this: In the absence of the built-in restraints that would accompany an office, what defines the outer limits of a big man's behavior? How much control, for instance, can a big man exert over others with divara? If, in other words, what it is to be a big man cannot be separated from what a big man does, it is also true that what it is to be a big man cannot be separated from what a big man cannot do. During a mortuary ceremony—most specifically during a matamatam—a statement is made about just what a big man can and cannot do. The matamatam is a proving ground for a big man; at this time he demonstrates that he does control followers and that he does control the tubuan. But the matamatam also defines what a big man cannot do by showing that he, as well as everyone else, is limited by the power of the tubuan, and especially the power of the tubuan's court, the kilung court. It is appropriate that such a statement be made at a mortuary ceremony in which former big men are excluded from public consciousness through the activities of their successors.

The meaning of the matamatam lies not only in its activities but also in the sequence of these activities. This latter aspect is particularly important in understanding the meaning implicit in the juxtaposition of the dukduk and tubuan. It is significant that the kumbak during which the dukduk is of central importance is preceded and followed by the parts of the matamatam in which the tubuan is paramount.

For these reasons I will present the events of the matamatam in their sequence, although this sequence is in part a reconstruction: I will describe certain preparations which I saw on Karavar for a matamatam completed in 1969 after we left. I will then describe a number of intermediate steps based on informants' accounts and on observations I made in 1972 of another matamatam. Finally I will describe the concluding portions of the matamatam I witnessed during 1968 on the neighboring island of Utuan. In actuality the Utuan matamatam occurred before the Karavarans began their preparations in 1968, so some of the events and some of the people participating in the Karavaran preparations were determined by alliances established at the earlier Utuan matamatam. Thus I will not be able to follow particular big men all the way through the sequence, and, although I will be able to describe specific stages as they actually occurred, the overall pattern will have to be somewhat generalized.

The preliminary activities in a matamatam indicate who the sponsors are and whether they can act as big men. These activities are an introductory statement about the nature and the means of order. In these early stages big men order the activities of their followers—and others as well—by directing and financing certain minor ceremonies. They also impose a more general kind of order on the community as a whole. Members of both moieties are exhorted to cease their aimless existence and focus their efforts on getting divara to meet the expenses of the forthcoming matamatam. The community as a whole is committed to the order of the sequence of activities that compose the matamatam. Even the dead are conceptually ordered as the sponsors each declare which dead they take as their responsibility.

These preliminary steps have the same purposes as the matamatam proper, although these purposes are pursued less intensively than they are later when a tubuan is constructed. At this earlier time, only part of the social activity is directed toward the matamatam; later, all activity focuses on it.

In late 1967, shortly before our arrival, three Karavaran big men of the Pikalambe moiety decided to sponsor a matamatam. They were Alipet, Ambo, and Tomerau. Of these, Alipet was clearly ascendant in ritual matters and in his possession of divara and cash. Alipet was an adept; Ambo and Tomerau were planning to become adepts at the next opportunity. Alipet was primarily in charge of the preparations, although he conferred frequently with Ambo and Tomerau.[2]

During a meeting at the taraiu, Alipet announced to the assembly of men that the Pikalambe moiety was ready to make a balanguan and therefore was reserving the forthcoming year. This announcement was not entirely surprising, since each of the principals had sounded out his followers to see if they could be prepared for the considerable expenditures in time and divara that would be required of them. In this way the Karavarans knew that a matamatam was planned although the actual timing of the announcement and of the matamatam itself perhaps came as a surprise to some.

Alipet's announcement caused excitement. The Karavarans consciously—and I would say correctly—regard a balanguan, and especially the matamatam, as their high point in life, the time when their social and cultural life is most intense. Furthermore, because it had been almost ten years

[2] Ambo and Tomerau were important men even though in 1968 neither had yet bought the tubuan. Much of their importance stemmed from their leadership in a kind of cargo cult business activity called the Kaun. Karavarans recognized that these two did not conform to the traditional definition of big man as adept, but nonetheless they considered them, along with Alipet, as the most important men of the Pikalambe moiety. Ambo bought the tubuan at the next opportunity, during 1970. Tomerau had planned to buy although he was unable to because of serious illness. Both Ambo and Tomerau did then subscribe to the traditional definition of big man.

since the Karavarans had last given a matamatam, a number
of young men were waiting to buy the dukduk, and a
number of dead had accumulated since the last balanguan
who needed to be finished.

The Karavarans were also eager to stage a matamatam to
gain intercommunity prestige. Although a matamatam is
regarded as the primary responsibility of one moiety, the
other moiety cooperates. Thus the entire community takes
great pride in the success of their matamatam. Success is
partly measured by the partnerships and alliances the sponsors establish with big men of other communities—political
relationships that determine to a great extent the nature of
political relations between their communities. Karavar, having been ritually quiescent for a number of years, was ready
to assert itself politically.

It was important for Alipet to make his announcement
publicly because the entire community must give its support
if a matamatam is to be successful. If men of both moieties
had been planning to sponsor a matamatam they would have
had to decide which should go first. Alipet was, in effect,
reserving the next matamatam for the Pikalambe moiety.
Since no members of the Maramar moiety were ready at that
time to sponsor a matamatam, his announcement was uncon-
tested.

After a particular ceremonial period has been claimed by a
moiety, the first step is to allocate the dead for whom the
mortuary ceremony is to be made. Any dead person, man,
woman, or a child, has many living kinsmen, some of whom
must take responsibility to have a cement gravestone made
for him. During the matamatam we witnessed on Karavar,
all the Pikalambes who had died since the last balanguan had
cement gravestones made for them.

In determining who should make a gravestone for a deceased kinsman, relationships had to be balanced one against another. Although a father would make the gravestones for his children who had died when young, usually matrilineal ties were more important than patrilateral in determining mortuary obligations. Thus a dead man would have a gravestone made for him by his sister's son rather than by his son, unless his son were especially important. On Karavar there was only one gravestone made during this period for a man whose son was alive and active. This was for Lokompot who had died when his two sons, Tanglik and William, were small. Although members of Lokompot's liting had made a balanguan for him years before, no gravestone had been constructed—for what reasons I do not know. In 1968, in preparation for the matamatam, it was appropriate that a gravestone be made for him. There was a slight altercation about who would take responsibility for it. Tomerau, one of Lokompot's liting mates, made a gravestone for Lokompot without consulting Tanglik and William, who then claimed that they were ready to buy the cement and make the gravestone and that Tomerau had infringed on their interests. Tanglik justified to me his desire to make a gravestone for his father by using a standard argument: he and Lokompot were of one blood and if it had not been for Lokompot, Tanglik would not have existed. The dispute was settled easily: Tanglik, who was not a person of ambition or influence, and Tomerau agreed that Tanglik should just pay a share of the divara given to the workmen. The settlement conformed to the usual arrangement in which a son cooperates with his father's liting but allows them to carry the primary mortuary responsibility.

The sponsors, Alipet, Ambo, and Tomerau, unlike the

less important Pikalambes, did none of the actual work of making the gravestones. Instead they hired a work force consisting mainly of Maramar men, experienced in carpentry, who made the wooden forms and cast the cement. The work first took place next to Ambo's house.

Alipet, Ambo, and Tomerau were conspicuous supervisors, but Tomiton, the next most important man to Ambo in his liting, was prominent too. Considerable friction had already developed between Ambo and Tomiton. Ambo was rather puritan in his outlook, valuing hard work, sobriety, and public responsibility, whereas Tomiton lived riotously. Tomiton was the only member of his and Ambo's liting, however, who had purchased the rights to make the tubuan that would be necessary at the coming matamatam. Thus Tomiton was rather important in the proceedings even though he was distinctly subordinate to Ambo in prestige and took a much smaller share of the financial burden.

The gravestones made the first day were for Ambo and Tomiton's mother's brother, Tokoikoi, who had been an extremely important man; for Ambo and Tomiton's mother's sister's son, Tilon; and for Tomiton's adult daughter, Iaprainde. Ambo, rather than Tomiton, took primary responsibility for the gravestones of the first two because these two were the more important of the deceased and Ambo was more important than Tomiton. Tomiton took care of the gravestone for his daughter, because his wife's liting, to which his daughter of course belonged, was sparsely represented on Karavar by only a few women. Ambo provided a midday meal of baked bananas and tapioca for everyone present—workers, supervisors, and bystanders.

The next day the same Maramar work force made gravestones, again at Ambo's house, for Karavar and Matuana, whom Tomerau claimed. Tomerau needed to finish someone in order to be a sponsor at the matamatam and thus further his political career. These two were the closest deceased kin he could muster. The way in which Tomerau traced his relationship to them shows the versatile way in which kinship is customarily used: After the death of Tomerau's mother, his father married a woman who had borne Karavar and Matuana to a previous husband. Thus Tomerau could consider himself, Karavar, and Matuana to be siblings. This time Tomerau paid for the meal of rice and tinned fish served to those present at the work site.

The following day the newly cast gravestones were erected in the cemetery.[3] Karavar is divided geographically into named halves—Rakukur and Romolot—a division that used to have major significance when each half had a government-appointed luluai. Although there is now only one luluai for all of Karavar and this division appears today in only a few

[3] While watching the work in the cemetery, Tomerau suggested a new procedure for burial and grave marking to Ambo, Alipet, and me. He suggested that in the future two tall obelisks be constructed, one for the Maramars and the other for the Pikalambes, which would stand in the village itself near the church, rather than in the woods where the present cemeteries were located. Each obelisk would have a bronze plaque and on the plaque would be inscribed the names of the dead of that moiety, with the most senior at the top. In that way people could see who their ancestors were. All the Pikalambes and all the Maramars would be buried in two common graves near each shaft with one grave for each moiety. Tomerau told me that he got this idea from the Kokopo war memorial and also from a newly erected war memorial in Rabaul that had attracted a great deal of Karavaran interest. There does seem to be a tremendous preoccupation with mortuary affairs in this culture. We were asked many times during this period when the gravestones were being made whether this procedure was the same as that followed in America.

activities, each half still maintains a separate cemetery. As the work progressed in the Rakukur cemetery on Tomerau, Ambo, and Tomiton's half of the island, two visitors, Doti and Takaru, appeared from the neighboring island of Utuan. These two men had been among the principals at a matamatam on Utuan several weeks before. At this earlier matamatam, gifts had been given to Alipet by Takaru and to Ambo by Doti, and a return presentation would be made by Alipet and Ambo when the Karavarans completed their own matamatam. Ambo and Alipet as well as Tomerau and several other Karavarans had been singled out for special gifts because the news was abroad that the Pikalambes of Karavar were ready to begin a matamatam. During the period while these debts were outstanding, there was an intercommunity alliance between donor and recipient. That was why Doti and Takaru stopped by Karavar to show interest in their allies' ritual activities and why they were given a special welcome.

Casting the gravestones followed much the same pattern on the other half of the island. There, Alipet's house was the main center of activity. Alipet had gravestones made for his mother and his mother's sister as well as for several of his children who had died when quite young.

By the time the sponsors' gravestones were made and placed in the cemetery, a number of other people of lesser importance were making gravestones for their own kin. They did their own work or worked in small teams, instead of paying others to work for them as befits a sponsor. In the next few days there was a flurry of gravestone construction in the two cemeteries on both ends of the island, a great deal of speculation about what death dates to put on the gravestones, and in some cases confusion as to where a specific individual

had been buried.[4] (I saw in 1968 one gravestone carrying a
death date of 1972, so it is unlikely that the gravestones could
give much useful demographic information.)

During this period of cementing, Alipet, Ambo, and Tomerau met privately on frequent occasions. At one such
meeting they agreed on the amount of divara each would give
the principal Maramar workers who had made their gravestones. Each was to contribute the same amount. The payments for the gravestones were made eleven days after the
cement casting began (May 20 to May 31). On the final day,
both men and women assembled in back of Ambo's house,
which had been the center for much of the cement casting.
The women, as usual, were seated off to the side but were
clearly present. With Alipet, Ambo, and Tomerau in the
lead and carrying the largest contributions of divara, all the
Pikalambes as a group took divara and packages of cooked
food to those Maramars who had worked on the gravestones.
A presentation of divara and food is the usual compensation
for nonritual services such as stringing divara or building a
canoe and for ritual services such as constructing a tubuan.
Then this group of Pikalambes placed divara in two piles
near a large quantity of food, most of which had been purchased by Alipet, Ambo, and Tomerau. One pile of divara
was for the women of the Rakukur half of Karavar and the
other for the women of the Romolot half in payment for their
having cooked this food. Next, all of the Maramars brought

---

[4] Several people dreamed that the dead for whom the gravestones had
just been made were happy with their new houses—that is, their cement
gravestones. These were described as *ruma na kapa*, which means a house
that has European-style corrugated iron roofing, fibro-cement walls, and
a cement floor. Such a house is beyond the means of all but the wealthiest
of the Duke of Yorkers.

divara over to Ambo and Alipet in order to help them with their expenses.[5] Finally, just before the men and women ate in their separate groups, some of the women who had carried sand and gravel from the beach to be used in the cement mixture, began to complain that they too should have been given divara for their help in making the gravestones. Ambo and several others then went to the women's section and distributed divara to them.

The last episode—that of giving divara to some of the women—should be related to another incident occurring shortly afterward. After the meal was finished, a number of the younger men who regarded Alipet as their big man and were in his apik quietly walked off before the after-dinner speeches. Although not part of the Maramar work crew, they had helped with the cement casting and therefore felt that they should be paid. Wilson, our cook, was one of these disgruntled young men. He later told me that he was particularly upset because he had just expended a very generous three fathoms of divara as his share in the general Pikalambe contribution to the Maramar workers. He and the other young men had been expecting to recoup some of their losses by being in turn paid for their own work.

Alipet ignored the claims of his young male followers, perhaps because he felt that since they were dependent on him he could get by without paying them. The women who had grumbled loudly at being overlooked in the distribution of divara had a stronger position of leverage than did the young men because they were willing to make a public

[5] The manner of assistance in this case has a parallel in a funeral ceremony at which time close matri– and patri–kin of the deceased are given lengths of divara by all the rest of the men present in order to assist them in their forthcoming general distribution of divara.

scene. As a consequence they were paid by Ambo and the other members of Ambo's apik. Ambo was known for a more consistent if unspectacular generosity than was Alipet, whose reputation rested on his well-timed public displays of largesse.

Following the meal came the speeches. As the most eminent man of the Pikalambe moiety, Alipet began. He said that this day was the first step in expending lots of divara. The Maramars knew what they were to do—they were to help the Pikalambes by following their wishes. Then he went on to compare the Karavarans to a flock of chickens that stay together when small but then as adults separate and go every which way. This was not good. Instead they all should be like a school of fish that stick together and follow their leader. The forthcoming work would not be difficult if all would pull together.

Part of this speech in favor of unity was directed against three rather important Pikalambes who had been absent when the gravestones were made and only one of whom was present to help with the distribution of divara this final day. These three, mentioned earlier, had been making preliminary arrangements to purchase the right to make a tubuan from a mother's brother on the neighboring island of Mioko. Their activities caused quite a bit of concern among the prominent men on Karavar for several reasons. One reason was that Mioko was in a continual state of rivalry with Karavar on a whole range of issues. Another was that the men were displaying potentially threatening political ambition. Alipet thus had grounds for criticizing their divisive behavior in his analogy of the individualistic chickens.

Ambo spoke next about the forthcoming balanguan. He said that the Karavarans had led a pointless and undirected existence for some years, forgetful of the customs of the past. They were not free of obligation. All those dead yet to be finished were still a heavy responsibility. The slate must be cleared with divara so that the living would be free (*langa langa*) again. Then Ambo, like Alipet, also criticized the men who had been absent arranging to buy the tubuan at Mioko.

Making the gravestones is the first stage in the cycle of activities comprising a matamatam. The next step is to build the small houses that will lodge the tubuan and dukduk figures. A house is built at the specific taraiu of each of the sponsors who have purchased the right to make a tubuan. In the forthcoming matamatam at Karavar, only two houses would be made: one at Alipet's taraiu and one at Tomiton and Ambo's taraiu.

The houses at the taraiu are built in quite traditional fashion, directly on the ground and with roofing of kunai grass. They have thatched roofs rather than the more modern corrugated iron roofs because, I was told, the traditional grass roof requires a great deal of labor for its construction.[6] Young men of both moieties are paid for collecting and bringing in the thatching from its source on a neighboring island and then paid again for tying the thatching onto the roof. As is usual in ceremonial payments, the sponsors of the mortuary ceremony lead in the payment of the workers and give larger portions of divara than do their supporters who follow them.

Once the thatched houses are built, large bunches of green

---

[6] The pattern here of maximizing the opportunity for public expenditure is present in many parts of Melanesia. One well-documented account can be found in Oliver's description of the construction of a Solomon Island men's club house (1955:372–379).

bananas are hung up inside to ripen. When the bananas are ripe they are presented along with a gift of cooked food, a package of betel nuts and one fathom of divara to various men, both of the local and of outside communities. This gift asks the recipient to join in an exchange relationship with the sponsors of the matamatam by contributing either a dukduk or a tubuan.

There are many ways during a matamatam in which favors may be exchanged and debts and obligations created between big men and between big men and lesser men. These ceremonial exchanges constitute the principal means by which interisland and intraisland alliances are established; an aspiring man acquires prestige by being accepted or singled out as an exchange partner by an established big man. A man entering into an alliance risks severe criticism, however, if he does not appropriately reciprocate all the gifts and hospitality.

The sponsors of the matamatam often decide together which alliances each will establish. Thus there is a pairing of a particular sponsor and particular recipient. The recipients must be carefully selected. A recipient who contributes a dukduk or a tubuan upon invitation must later be repaid with a dukduk or a tubuan when the recipient himself holds a mortuary ceremony. Hence the sponsor's invitation initiates a fairly long term obligation for both parties. Although it is flattering to be singled out by an important man from either the local or an outside community with such an invitation, acceptance commits the recipient to substantial expenditures of divara and cash. He must not only feed and pay his work crew for making the dukduk or tubuan but he is expected prominently to help the sponsors in their distribution of divara. A man may be reluctant to participate in another's balanguan either because he may be short of divara or because he is saving for some major production of his own. Nevertheless a man could be embarrassed to refuse such an invitation because such refusal might indicate that he is not rich enough to accept and furthermore does not have sufficient followers to help him. On the other hand, if such an overture is refused by a clearly acknowledged big man it might be interpreted as implying that the man issuing the invitation was presumptuous. I know that one such invitation at the Utuan matamatam was not offered to Alipet because it was known that he was planning his own balanguan and therefore might refuse to get involved in another one. Sometimes to avoid awkwardness a big man may first be asked informally whether he wishes to receive a formal invitation.

Preparations for a matamatam do not necessarily move along briskly step by step. Sometimes there is a long interval between the construction of the gravestones and other early preparations and the final portion—the construction of tubuans and dukduks. For the matamatam I witnessed at Utuan, the houses at the taraiu had been built some three or four years before. Men pointed to intervening events to explain the delay: there had been deaths, funerals, and matamatams in other communities as well as events of a seasonal nature such as Christmas and Easter celebrations which had taken the divara and time of the sponsors and their followers. Predictions were being made at the time I left the field in December 1968 that the Karavaran matamatam would be delayed as well. The reasoning was that several close kinsmen of Ambo and Alipet had died and it would be necessary for these two big men to divert divara from the anticipated matamatam to provide for the funerals. Neither of these big men did in fact expend a great deal on these funerals and I strongly suspect that sponsors are not averse to postponing their matamatams. Such postponements advertise the multifold nature of their commitments as well as keep them in the public eye. Someone could be described as being "ready" to give a matamatam for several years, and such delays, if there were good excuses, would, I think, simply enhance a sponsor's name, as long as the hint of insolvency could be avoided. (The Karavaran Pikalambe matamatam was, in fact, given on schedule during 1969.)

As the final stages of the matamatam approach, the entire community is exhorted to focus all of its efforts on preparation. At almost any public meeting during this time the big men are likely to urge their fellows—especially the young men—to be "strong" in accumulating divara.[7] They will say that money is a matter of no account while divara is everything.

There are rather standard ways of getting divara. One is to purchase tobacco, biscuits, or other minor luxury items with cash in Rabaul and then sell them for divara in the village. This kind of conversion goes on all the time for big men and their wives, as well as for many others; however, I think that there may be some general flurry of these minor transactions to prepare for a specific event such as a matamatam.

Other procedures exist for raising divara for specific oc-

[7] Since young men are always being harangued by their elders, I asked some of the older informants whether such exhortations to work hard and acquire lots of divara were directed at them when they were young. They said that such had been the case. The older men had given them advice about the various "paths" (*akepi*) to divara—assiduous gardening and planting foods that were likely to be in short supply on other islands, for example. Lectures to the young men encouraging them to work industriously are understood as a normal part of the relationship between the generations. The young men were blasé about the lectures. One told me that the older men were always criticizing the young men simply because the young men had physical vigor and the older men were jealous.

casions. One was followed by an old man of the Maramar moiety who was planning to give a matamatam after the Karavaran Pikalambes had finished theirs. For several years he had been earning divara by restringing short lengths of divara belonging to other people into strands of standard length. As payment, he received ten to twenty per cent of the divara he had strung.

Divara can be collected through a credit arrangement whereby foodstuffs are exchanged at a very favorable rate for divara. Such a transaction includes a proviso that the parties will later exchange the asymmetrical roles of donor and recipient. Therefore, on a long-term basis no profit is made on either side although divara can be raised to attain immediate goals.

Another means of acquiring divara is generally reserved for big men. On Karavar there was a small diesel-powered workboat under Ambo's control, although it was supposed to be the property of a cargoistic business enterprise called the "Kaun." [8] For festive occasions this boat transported men and women to neighboring islands. Or in bad weather it transported the Karavaran women to the neighboring island of Ulu where the Karavaran gardens were located. Either Ambo himself, or another big man operating with his permission, collected fares in divara from the passengers. If, for example, Tomerau chartered this boat, he paid Ambo one dollar in cash for the trip to Ulu and then received a total of several fathoms of divara as payment from the passengers. This rate of exchange was much more favorable than the rate of exchange when trade tobacco, for example, was purchased with money and then sold for divara.

Still another favorable way of converting money into di-

[8] The Kaun is described in Errington (1974).

vara was under Tomerau's jurisdiction. Tomerau, as Karavar's leading church elder, had a certain control over the
divara given as Sunday-morning offerings. These offerings
were stored in bottles, later to be sold at a bargain rate for
money which then went to the church. Tomerau himself
bought most of these bottles, although he allowed a few
others to have a turn. There was some grumbling about
Tomerau's virtual monopoly, but most accepted his behavior
as typical of the way a big man operates and hence in the nature of things.

A matamatam requires not only divara but—as is the case
throughout Melanesia—large quantities of food. Often Melanesians must make special provisions to collect large quantities of food for consumption by the guests and for the ceremonial presentations. Frequently special gardens are planted
in anticipation of the ceremony. Such preparations are not
the case, however, in the Duke of York Islands.

This anomaly can, in part, be explained by the growing
requirements of the essential ceremonial food, taro. Taro, to
be grown successfully in the Duke of York Islands, at least in
the opinion of the inhabitants, must be planted on land
freshly cleared from virgin jungle or on land that has been
fallow a sufficient time for large trees to have matured. Not
only is a huge amount of labor required to clear this kind of
bush, there is hardly any such land remaining. Rather than
rely on locally grown taro for a feast, a Duke of York ceremonial sponsor will purchase with cash what he needs from
the Tolai markets in either Rabaul or Kokopo.

Ceremonial meals may also include coconuts, bananas, fish
and sweet potatoes, for which the local supply is usually adequate. These foods are purchased by the sponsor with divara, and the actual payment for them may be part of the

ceremony. A sponsor pays others to produce the feast food for the same reason that he pays others to construct the gravestones and the thatched house at his taraiu: to demonstrate his ability to impose order. He is ordering the activities of those who do the actual work as well as the activities of his followers who assist him in paying the workers. The entire matamatam is an opportunity for the sponsor to demonstrate his wealth and his power.

CHAPTER 6

Initial Stages in the Utuan Matamatam

Current Political Relations

A major ceremony such as a matamatam is an "international" event in that big men from the surrounding communities attend. Part of the definition of a big man is that the big men of other communities accept him as such. At a matamatam or some other major mortuary ceremony with an influx of distinguished guests, therefore, a man can best prove himself to be a big man. Because a community has a strong sense of solidarity and a big man is identified with a particular community, interaction between big men both reflects and determines the political relationships current between their respective communities. Part of the necessary background for events of the Utuan matamatam is the political situation existing between various communities.

Political relations follow the pattern of situationally determined oppositions. This is the familiar notion that a group is solidary only in opposition to another group of the same order. From the Karavaran view, Karavar as a community was markedly superior to Utuan in such things as conformity to traditional practices, munificence on ceremonial occasions, adherence to United Church practices such as Sunday abstention from drinking. In wider contexts, Utuan and Karavar were superior to Mioko and her allies; the Duke of York

Islanders as a group were superior to the Tolai of New Britain; and the Duke of York Islanders plus the Tolai were superior to the people of mainland New Guinea. But the critical political division in this series of oppositions was between Karavar and Utuan on one hand and Mioko, with a variable cluster of allies, on the other.

At the time of our visit, the principal idiom in which this division was expressed and justified concerned membership in the administration-sponsored Local Government Council. Mioko and a neighboring ally, Mualim, were the principal Duke of York communities that had joined the Council. Both were also Catholic enclaves in the overwhelmingly United Church Duke of York Islands. Karavar and Utuan, in contrast, were centers of the anti-Council movement called the Kaun. Followers of the Kaun and of the Council saw themselves as fundamentally opposed to each other because of their different positions vis-à-vis the administration. However, as one of Mioko's occasional allies against Karavar and Utuan is Inolo, which is Kaun, one suspects that the Kaun-Council distinction is the expression of, rather than the primary cause of, the rivalry.

One further preliminary: In order to make the ensuing description of the final and most important stages of the matamatam easier to follow, I offer a synopsis of the ritual events.

Synopsis of the Matamatam

The matamatam proper begins with a feast called *nangwan*, attended by all the men from the host community and all those men from neighboring communities who plan to take an active part in the matamatam. At this time the schedule of events is announced. During the days that follow, the men *kumbak*, which means that they seclude themselves from women at the taraiu, and the dukduks and tubuans are constructed. On a prearranged day, women from neighboring communities convene with the women of the host community to prepare ceremonial foods called *balabala*, which will form part of the later formal presentations of food and divara. They are paid immediately by the men for these services. During the next several nights women of the host community sing topical songs and are, again, paid by the men. They may be joined by groups of women from neighboring communities sent by some big man there who undertakes primary responsibility for their payment. The day after the balabala is prepared, construction work is completed on the dukduks and tubuans and the kumbak comes to an end. The day after the kumbak ends, the men with the dukduks and the tubuans emerge from the taraiu into the village. This is the climax of the matamatam, and groups of men from other communities come to participate as singers and drummers or only as bystanders. Such groups may arrive in a *kinivai*, that is, a flotilla of canoes escorting a tubuan. After the guests have arrived, each dukduk and tubuan is escorted individually onto the dancing ground in the village itself. A dancing ground is partially defined as such by the presence of a wooden slit gong and a *butur*, a leafy display stand upon which are placed such relics as minor personal effects of the deceased for whom the matamatam is being made, as well as large rolls of divara. After all the tubuans and dukduks have been individually presented, they are lined up and each is struck with divara by its owner. The striking of either tubuan or dukduk with divara is called *tutupur*. Following this there are exchanges and distributions of divara—acts of crucial social importance since it is at this time that both inter-

and intraisland alliances are established and big men seek to enhance their reputations. When these are concluded, the tubuans and dukduks dance to a male chorus of singers and drummers and then the men retire to the taraiu for a feast. At the taraiu, when all are assembled but just prior to the feast, the tubuans are ceremonially killed and their spirits released. The term for this final dispatch of the tubuans is *pupulung*. Several days later the tubuans and dukduks, now regarded as lifeless shells, make a final appearance in the village. They limp and straggle down the main village path, swishing flies away from each other as though from a corpse and acting moribund. Then they are physically dismantled and the men eat a final meal. This concludes the matamatam.

The Introduction to the Matamatam: the Nangwan Feast

The matamatam that I observed in May 1968 occurred on the neighboring island of Utuan. During April when I first heard about the preparations, it was referred to on Karavar— and on Utuan as well—as Doti's matamatam. Doti was one of the most important men on Utuan and probably the most important of the Maramars. Doti and his two partners were, however, by no means alone in sponsoring the matamatam. There were actually four groups of sponsors. Doti's was the core group and the most prestigious of the four; the other three groups of Maramar sponsors were said to have joined (*ruk*) with Doti's group. Each of these groups was able to maintain relative autonomy during the matamatam to the extent that each group was making its own balanguan for its deceased relatives. In this Utuan case, because of the eminence of each of the groups of sponsors involved, the matamatam was virtually a federation of separate balanguans. In other political contexts, a single group of sponsors might have been able to exercise a more central influence over all the proceedings of the matamatam. I suspect, for example, that the Karavaran matamatam would have shown more emphatically the domination of a single man—Alipet—than did the Utuan matamatam.

The Utuan matamatam had been delayed a number of years. The initial preparations, including the construction of the gravestones and the thatched houses at the taraius, had all taken place perhaps four years before the concluding portion of the matamatam in 1968. There were four such thatched houses, one at the taraiu of each group of sponsors. These houses had grown old but were still intact.

The final phase of the Utuan matamatam began on the first of May with the *nangwan*—the feast that signified to the Duke of York public that the last round of the matamatam was under way. The Utuan nangwan was in two parts. First there were feasts eaten concurrently at each of the four separate taraius of the four groups of sponsors. The men who attended the feast at each of these ceremonial centers were mainly those who would help construct the tubuans and the dukduks associated with that host group of sponsors. Immediately following this first set of feasts there was another nangwan at Doti's taraiu which everyone attended. The relationship among the four groups of sponsors, each with its separate taraiu ceremonial center, was shown by these two sets of feasts: the first defined each group of sponsors and their adherents as distinct; the second indicated that Doti and his partners were the most important of the four groups of sponsors.

Doti and his two cosponsors, Mesak and Koi, were the hosts at this second nangwan. All three men belonged to the same liting: Koi was Mesak's true mother's brother and Doti was Mesak's sister's son although his link to Mesak could not be traced precisely. There was, moreover, a tie of adoption between Mesak and Doti. Koi was an old man living on Mioko who had been a principal sponsor of a matamatam some years before but was now largely retired. Nevertheless, he was still shown great respect and accorded an honorary pre-eminence among the three cosponsors. All three—Doti, Koi, and Mesak—were adepts.

After the nangwan feast everyone remained seated until Koi stood up to wash his hands in the sea. This was one sign of respect accorded to Koi as the most illustrious of the adepts. After he had washed his hands, everyone else did likewise. Then Koi and Doti asked who had contributed food for the meal just concluded. As these individuals identified themselves, the sponsors from the four cooperating groups went in a body and paid each of them in divara. Koi then announced the schedule for the forthcoming matamatam so that the day when visitors would come was clearly understood. This was to be a Friday ten days away. On this day visitors would arrive in canoe flotillas and the tubuans and the dukduks would go into the village itself to be struck with divara. Another sponsor spoke saying that there should be no drinking of whiskey or methylated spirits on this particular Friday, although there could be drinking after the matamatam was finished.[1]

---

[1] This common injunction was ignored in practice. Not only did the younger men make their own arrangements for drink, but the big men often passed around drinks to the younger men who were singing and drumming for the dancing tubuans and dukduks as well as to their peers. This was all part of the theme of conspicuous hospitality. The reason, however, for the objections voiced about drinking at these ceremonies was a real fear that some of the secrets of the tubuan might be inadvertently

Plate 1. Ambo speaking at nangwan

revealed to the women. The most likely calamity was that the tubuan carrier would fall and the top—the mask—would come loose and reveal that the figure did come apart. Although all men who carry the figures knew that if they slipped and fell for whatever reason they were to hold on firmly to the component pieces so that the figure stayed intact, there was danger that coordination and judgment might be impaired by drink.

One of the final speakers was Ambo from Karavar, who, as I have said, had a prominent role in the Kaun. The Kaun attempted to emulate European business practices so that European profits might result. One of the reasons, in Ambo's view, why Europeans are successful in business and have factories and material wealth is that they work hard and do not just lounge about as do the New Guineans. Ambo had developed something akin to the Protestant ethic and opposed drinking and idleness. It was not surprising then that in his speech he advocated that the matamatam be kept as brief as possible. (A matamatam can be considerably prolonged if any of the sponsors wish to make a particularly conspicuous display. In these cases certain tubuans may be kept "alive" several weeks after the other tubuans have been ritually killed. The matamatam then lingers on to be concluded with another feast.)

In all of these speeches, a speaker began by greeting the village luluai and the big men present. He did not mention any by name but just said, "Greetings to the luluai and all the big men." However, many of the speakers also included a general greeting to all of the *varvangala* present. The varvangala, a man's patrilateral descendants, do not form any discrete group; the term just refers to people who in certain contexts consider themselves to be descendants of a particular male. There is during a mortuary ceremony an emphasis on the cooperation of those who really are the kindred of the deceased; these of course include individuals of both moieties and of different communities.

The nangwan is the only occasion I know of in which the purchase of food is made at the feast itself—usually the sponsor of a feast will purchase the necessary food privately. Possibly this display of munificence is intended to provide an

Plate 2. Ambo, Doti, Otia, Tomiton, and Alipet—some of the Karavaran and Utuan big men

impressive opening to the final stages of the matamatam at a time when important visitors are present. Although in both the prior and the subsequent portions of the matamatam some services are in fact not paid for, at least during the nangwan the impression is presented that the ideal of paying for all services in a mortuary ceremony is being observed.

Only eleven Karavarans out of an adult male population of about forty went to Utuan for either feast. Three of these men belonged to Doti's liting; three were in the liting of a man named Takaru, a Maramar who cooperated closely with Doti in a wide range of activities and who was contributing a dukduk to the Doti balanguan as his portion of the matamatam; one, Kepas, was the true son of a deceased man for whom one of the groups was making a balanguan. Several other Karavarans told me they went simply because they were Maramars, an entirely acceptable reason since there is nothing exclusive about the nangwan. Both Ambo and Alipet went as the principal representatives of the Karavaran community, even though neither had close kinship connections with the balanguan sponsors. Of this group of Karavarans, only two of the six Karavaran adepts attended. One of these was Kongkong, a full brother of Takaru who cooperated with him on his dukduk; the other was Alipet, the acknowledged leader of the Karavaran adepts.

Two important adepts from Karavar were absent. One was Tonga, who was in a political decline: he had spent virtually all of his divara on an impressive series of mortuary ceremonies in the late 1950's. He was the senior adept, respected and feared for his knowledge of magic but otherwise regarded as a crotchety old man. He had no children and had alienated his matri-kin by his autocratic ways.[2] Several of my

[2] Tonga's case is interesting, since it shows the fate that may await a big man once the foundations of his power have disappeared. One critical breach in his relations with his sister's sons occurred some years after he had already dissipated most of his divara. Tonga was simultaneously married to two women, a situation by that time somewhat unusual. He decided to divorce both of these women and marry yet another. A divorce at the man's instigation requires the considerable expenditure of one hundred fathoms of divara for each wife who is repudiated. Remarriage would require payment of the bride price for a new wife. The total for all this would have been around 250 fathoms, a great deal of divara. His classificatory sister's son, Twembe, was flatly unwilling to provide the requisite divara, especially since he found no fault with either of Tonga's wives and thought that Tonga was under the delusion that he was still a young blade. Other incidents of this sort also alienated Tonga from his junior apik members. Thus Tonga at the time of our study was something of an outcast who was still trying to exercise authority over his apik without having the resources of divara necessary for full control.

informants thought that Tonga did not attend the nangwan because he was afraid he might at this time be given the bananas, betel nut, cooked food, and fathom of divara that constitute an invitation to make a tubuan or a dukduk. Such an invitation, as mentioned earlier, is usually given at the time the thatched houses are built at the taraius, but the nangwan also provides an opportunity for last-minute invitations. Without divara and the support it brings, Tonga would have suffered the embarrassment of having to reject the invitation.

The other prominent Karavaran adept who did not go was Luloi. Luloi was planning his own mortuary ceremony, and my informants thought perhaps he could not afford to be drawn into the Utuan matamatam. (Luloi did give a very modest balanguan during 1971. He constructed one tubuan and did not solicit any dukduks. He used Alipet's house at the taraiu rather than construct his own.)

Kinship: Sponsors, Followers, and Allies

During the week following that nangwan, the dukduks and tubuans were constructed at the taraius. Each of the four groups of sponsors had their followers construct a tubuan; the allies of these sponsors had their own followers construct a dukduk. Although I had been told that such an ally could contribute either a dukduk or a tubuan, the tubuan is to a great extent the prerogative of the sponsor; the dukduks are, in contrast, made as an embellishment to the matamatam. It is advantageous to the sponsor or sponsors of a mortuary ceremony to have allies make dukduks since a mortuary ceremony acquires the prestige of a matamatam only with the presence of dukduks. If a man is to sponsor a matamatam, he must already be of sufficient importance so that other important men will be willing to contribute dukduks.

The relationships between the various members of a group of sponsors and between a group of sponsors and its cluster of followers and between the group of sponsors and its allies who contribute the dukduks are all expressed in kinship terms. The following genealogies which I collected at the Utuan matamatam are expressions of local patterns of cooperation and alliance.

The principal group of sponsors, as I have mentioned, was composed of Doti, Mesak, and Koi. They were making their portion of the matamatam for two deceased adepts, Talenganai and Tokumat, and for a woman, Ialita. Figure 4 is their schematic genealogy.

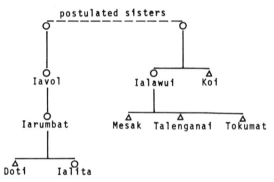

Figure 4. Genealogy of the Doti, Mesak, Koi group

The specific genealogical connection between the two lines of descent shown in Figure 4 is not known; such gaps are common since genealogies tend to be very short.[3] It is difficult to know the original reasons for the conjunction of Doti

---

[3] We knew of two adults who were unable to remember their own mother's names because their mothers had died when they were young and they were reared by adoptive mothers.

and Mesak's lines. The two women at the apex of the genealogy may in fact have been true sisters, or perhaps they were
considered to be sisters because one was adopted by the
mother of the other or both were adopted by yet another
woman. Since the litings and apiks are focused on particular
big men, as these big men come and go there is a redistribution of people and their genealogies around new focal
points.

The Doti-Mesak-Koi group occupied the taraiu belonging
to Doti. The tubuan made by this group had been owned
by Talenganai, one of the deceased adepts being finished by
them. It is customary for each group of sponsors to make one
tubuan, and if one of the deceased for whom they are making
their balanguan was an adept, then they will make his own
tubuan.[4] If no one of the deceased was an adept, they will
make the tubuan of one of the sponsors.

Doti, Mesak, and Koi directed the construction of their
tubuan. Although I do not know everyone who worked on
their tubuan, some of the final touches were provided by two
young men, Jek and Robin, who were general helpers at this
taraiu. In addition to working on the tubuan these two did
chores such as sweeping and cooking, for which they were
paid with divara. Jek had been adopted by Doti, and Robin,
by Mesak. The prestige of both Doti and Mesak was indicated by their full utilization of the potentialities of the
adoptive relationship.

The only group of sponsors to whom allies, each with his
separate work crew, contributed dukduks was that of Doti-

---

[4] Although an adept is thought to be very happy if his own tubuan is
made and appears before him on his death bed, there is no belief that he is
similarly pleased if his tubuan appears at the balanguan in which he is
finished.

Mesak-Koi. Of the seven contributors, five were volunteering their dukduks as *marawut* (help) and two were responding to earlier formal invitations with dukduks as *dinau* (debt). The reasons these five men were giving dukduks as marawut were given me in terms of kinship. Of these five, only two had any genealogically close ties with the group of sponsors. One of these, Takaru, was married to the actual daughter of Talenganai, one of the men being finished by the Doti-Mesak-Koi group of sponsors. Since Mesak was Talenganai's brother, Takaru was considered Mesak's son-in-law and, I was told, he was making a dukduk for this reason. Since Takaru and Doti cooperated in almost all activities, however, reasons for Takaru's participation other than his relationship with Mesak could have been found. Another man, Orim, contributed a dukduk because he was married to one of Doti's actual sisters. The remaining three of this group were Dariut, a patrilateral descendant of Talenganai; Tomat, a classificatory brother-in-law of Talenganai; and Buka, a classificatory brother-in-law of Mesak. The genealogical relationship between each of these three and the Doti-Mesak-Koi group was exceedingly vague.

The two who contributed dukduks as dinau were Pitai and Toweina. Pitai was the leading member of the Utuan adepts, the *tene tubuan;* his dukduk had to be repaid when and if Pitai himself sponsored a balanguan. Toweina made a dukduk in return for a dukduk that Mesak had made for him previously.

All of the contributors of the dukduks, with the exception of Takaru, were Pikalambes, and thus of the moiety opposite to that of the sponsors. The matamatam is the primary responsibility of one moiety; the other moiety has a secondary role of assistance. For this reason it is appropriate that the sponsors make tubuans and their allies of the opposite moiety help them with dukduks. Tubuans are associated with big men, prestige and power; dukduks in contrast are much less associated with the exercise of political power and in fact in the context of the matamatam may be referred to as flowers (*purpur*)—as embellishments. Moreover, the association of the dukduk with cooperative relations between moieties—as between father and son—makes it an appropriate figure to serve as the symbol and the medium of the cooperative relationship between the sponsors of one moiety and their allies of the other.

The matamatam sponsors whom the Doti-Mesak-Koi group regarded as second in importance to themselves were Dengit and Alipati. These two were finishing Atu and Tomti, both of whom had been adepts. The tubuan they made was Atu's. The relationship between these principals is shown in Figure 5.

Alipati, who was from the Duke of York Island and therefore not from Utuan, and Dengit were classificatory mother's brother and sister's son; Alipati was the senior of the two, an adept and a very wealthy man both in divara and money.

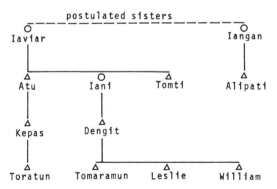

Figure 5. Genealogy of the Dengit, Alipati group

Dengit was not an adept and was of only slightly above-average importance. As the dominant sponsor and as an adept, Alipati's presence was essential for this balanguan. The work force was composed of Kepas and Toratun, both Karavarans and patrilateral descendants of Atu; Dengit's three sons; plus three other Maramars who were said to be helping simply because they were Maramars and because they, like other helpers, would be given divara for their assistance.

At this same taraiu occupied by Dengit and Alipati and their work force, another group of men was also making a tubuan which belonged to Lipan, a youngish adept, probably in his early forties. The social composition of this group of workers, the reason they were making a tubuan at all, and their choice of a construction site were explained to me in the following way.

This particular tubuan was made by two pairs of full brothers: Lipan and Eron, and Kindor and Timet. The fathers of each of these pairs of brothers were themselves full brothers and were named Tokumat and Toyung. Tokumat and Toyung, moreover, were full brothers with Talenganai and Mesak. Both Tokumat and Talenganai were being finished by the Doti-Mesak-Koi group. (Toyung had been finished sometime in the past.) Thus Lipan, Eron, Kindor, and Timet, all relatively young men, wished to assist in the balanguan for Tokumat and Talenganai who were father or father's brother to all four of them. If there had not been a further complicating factor, these four would have been associated with the Doti-Mesak-Koi camp. However, after Toyung died, his widow and the mother of Lipan and Eron married Tomti. Thus Lipan and Eron became Tomti's stepchildren. Kindor and Timet, whose mother did not remarry, followed along with Lipan and Eron in their new relationship with Tomti. Their relationship with Tomti was significant in this Utuan matamatam because Tomti, along with Atu, was being finished by the Dengit-Alipati group. That Lipan's tubuan was made not only for Tokumat and Talenganai but for Tomti and Atu as well, was demonstrated because Lipan's tubuan was constructed at the same taraiu where Dengit and Alipati were making their tubuan for Tomti and Atu.

Lipan and his brothers were Pikalambes and their tubuan was thus a Pikalambe tubuan. It is unusual for Pikalambes to construct a tubuan at a Maramar matamatam. A more customary procedure for Lipan and his group would have been to join the work crew of either the Doti-Mesak-Koi group or of the Dengit-Alipati group. Another alternative would have been for them to contribute a dukduk to either group of sponsors. If a nonsponsor were to make a tubuan, it might be thought that he was trying to eclipse the sponsors at their own matamatam. I can only suggest that the tortuous genealogical explanation that Lipan and his brothers offered was to define themselves not as sponsors, which would have been impossible at a Maramar matamatam, nor as mere helpers, in which case a dukduk would have been an appropriate contribution, but as something in between. By stressing their special relations with two sets of deceased, Lipan and his brothers presented themselves as quasi-sponsors. It is my conjecture, then, that their elaborate chain of reasoning enabled them to have the importance of constructing a tubuan without making a direct challenge to the prestige of the big men who were sponsoring the matamatam.

At yet another taraiu, a tubuan was made under the sponsorship of Bangut, Minio, and Tande for a deceased woman

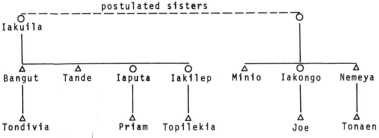

Figure 6. Genealogy of the Bangut, Minio, Tande group

named Iakongo. This tubuan was owned by Bangut. The
work force consisted of Tonaen, Joe, Priam, Kanem, Enry,
Tokumbur, Tondivia, and Topilekia. A surprisingly large
number of these appear on the genealogy in Figure 6. This
genealogy leaves out Tokumbur and Enry who were said to
be helping simply because they were Maramars, and Kanem,
a Pikalambe, who was said to be just helping out.

The tubuan was made explicitly for a woman. I think,
however, that if there had been close male kinsmen to be
finished, they would have been considered the focus of the
balanguan even though some women and children were to be
finished at the same time. For instance, I was at first told that
the Doti-Mesak-Koi group was making a balanguan for
Talenganai and Tokumat and only when I inquired in detail was the name of Doti's full sister, Ialita, included. In the
case of Bangut, Minio, and Tande, however, their sister,
Iakongo, was the major figure for whom the balanguan was
made.

The last of the four groups of sponsors was composed of
Mundiaro, Tomtun, and Tomitawa. They were making a
total of one dukduk and two tubuans for the matamatam. My
data on this group are incomplete since the group was centered on the neighboring island of Mioko and I was scarcely

aware of its existence during the early stages of the matamatam. Their case is interesting, though, since it shows the importance of adoption in both explaining and determining mortuary cooperation. The tubuan was made for Balawur and Iakalik. The relationships involved are presented in Figure 7.

Mundiaro explained to me his participation in this balanguan in the following way: Mundiaro, Tomtun, and Tomitawa had all been born on Mioko which is separated from Utuan by only a narrow channel. Iakalik, who was considered to be a "sister" of Iapatima and Iatinau, married on Utuan. She had no children and adopted Mundiaro, who went to live with her on Utuan. When a child is adopted by a childless couple, the adoptive parents will often take over the full range of parental responsibilities and the child itself will change its residence to live with its adoptive parents. This differs from the usual adoption in which the adoptive parents do not gain much control over the child. Although any child may participate in mortuary ceremonies made for his or her adoptive parents, it is most nearly obligatory in these relatively few cases in which responsibility for a child's upbringing has been taken over by the adoptive parents. Mundiaro thus did have a strong tie to his adoptive parents,

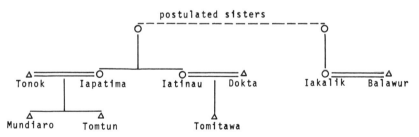

Figure 7. Genealogy of the Mundiaro, Tomtun, Tomitawa group

Iakalik and Balawur, a tie his brother Tomtun and his classificatory brother Tomitawa were willing to share. These
three had also collaborated in the past on mortuary ceremonies for Tonok, Iapatima, and Iatinau.

In the Utuan matamatam, Mundiaro seemed to be sid-
ing politically with Karavar and Utuan, where he had been
raised, against Mioko. This was shown in several ways: Mundiaro, who was contributing a dukduk to his own balanguan,
had his constructed in the Doti-Mesak-Koi camp on Utuan
while the others, Tomtun and Tomitawa, made their tubuans on Mioko. Mundiaro later used the tubuan of Doti-
Mesak-Koi rather than that of his brothers to visit ceremonially the Utuan cemetery of his adoptive mother Iakalik.
Furthermore, Mundiaro reputedly had asked his apik big
man, Tonga, to come from Karavar and assist him with
magic and advice during this matamatam.[5]

Political Relationships between Groups of Sponsors

I have listed the groups of sponsors, each of which was
making a balanguan as part of the overall matamatam, in the
order in which they were said to have joined with the core

[5] It was mentioned earlier that Tonga was an example of a big man
who with the expenditure of his divara had been reduced in many ways to
the status of a "rubbish man"; he had, however, maintained his autocratic
ways and a reputation for a superlative knowledge of dukduk-tubuan spells
and dancing magic. There had been ill feeling between Tonga and other
members of the apik including Mundiaro and Twembe for a number of
years, and when Mundiaro asked Tonga to assist him at the balanguan at
Utuan, Tonga refused. I was told that during the final portions of the matamatam, Mundiaro burst into tears saying that none of his big men had
come to see him. The conclusion of the Tonga-Mundiaro conflict occurred
the night Tonga died on Karavar. A message was sent to Mundiaro on
Utuan with instructions for him to pass the information on to his kinsmen
on Mioko, but he simply neglected to do it.

group of Doti, Mesak, and Koi. The four groups were not closely bound together, and, as I have indicated, the arrangement in certain respects was one of four separate balanguans occurring at the same place and time.

The relative independence of each group was shown in several ways. For example, each was centered in a particular taraiu and there was little visiting among the groups during the time the tubuans and dukduks were under construction. I was told that I was the only one who went freely from one area to another, and on these trips I was asked questions about the progress of construction at the various other camps.

Not only was each group of sponsors autonomous but there was often tension between one group and another. One rift began with a dispute over the butur—the display stand. According to a plan initially agreed upon by all four groups of sponsors, each group would have a separate butur in the hamlet of one member of the group of sponsors. Then later the relics and rolls of divara would be transferred to one major butur in Doti's hamlet where they would be displayed together. This would have been a pattern similar to that of the nangwan feasts. It would have given evidence that each of the four groups was distinct but would also have shown that the Doti-Mesak-Koi group was the most important, a conclusion which was, I think, generally accepted.

Doti tried to improve on this plan, however, by deciding that there was to be only one butur and that one at his hamlet. Here all four groups would be represented. Thus Doti was opposing the idea that the individual buturs should precede the main one and in effect denying the independence of the other three groups by making them appear wholly secondary to his own. Such an arrangement was not accepted by the other three groups of sponsors. They threatened instead to have only their separate buturs and their separate balanguans. In the face of such opposition, Doti reinstated the original plan.

Political Relationships between Sponsors and Allies

The ties established between individuals during the matamatam have considerable political importance both within and between communities. These ties can be established in a variety of ways. One way, already mentioned, is through the presentation of a formal invitation to make a dukduk. By giving such an invitation of betel nut, bananas, cooked food, and divara, the sponsors demonstrate that they regard the recipient as an established big man. The recipient will make a dukduk as dinau that will be considered part of the balanguan of this one particular group of sponsors. His tie will be with the sponsoring group as a whole, but within this group the particular sponsor whose divara was given in the invitation is the one responsible for repaying the dukduk on request. Thus, these formal invitations to participate with a dukduk in a balanguan involve donor and recipient in at least another round of cooperation. In the absence of such a formal invitation, however, it is still possible for someone to initiate the exchange with a sponsor. This was evident at the Utuan matamatam in which five men volunteered dukduks to the Doti-Mesak-Koi group as marawut.

There are other ways, as I learned from Tomerau, one of the Karavaran big men, that a man may help a sponsor in a balanguan. He may go during the night to a sponsor and give him a ten-fathom length of divara. Later when the sponsor is publicly striking his tubuan with divara he will employ the piece that has been loaned to him. The entire transaction will be a secret to the bystanders, who will think that this divara belonged to the sponsor. At a later time when the donor is giving a balanguan, the debt will be repaid in the same surreptitious way.[6] A volunteer may simply ask a sponsor what can be done to help him. The sponsor perhaps will suggest that the volunteer follow him in the distribution of divara that forms the concluding part of a balanguan. This is a convenient way for both men and women publicly to show generosity and support for their leaders without expending really substantial amounts of divara. It is one of the most efficient ways in which a follower may attract favorable attention from the big men and the people at large. Tomerau told me that during this distribution the big man will turn his head and see the follower and think: "True, I dissuaded him from making a dukduk but here he is helping me nevertheless." Since there are several distributions of this sort during a balanguan, the opportunity to help in this way is great.

Another method of providing help is for a man to go to the young men of his liting and tell them that they should prepare to make a dukduk. On the appointed day he and his followers will suddenly appear with this dukduk. And as the dukduk is escorted to the taraiu, he will give the customary introductory dance saying that he has come because he heard that the sponsor is giving a balanguan. This, said Tomerau, is what is done if a man feels that the sponsor has always

[6] The occasion for the repayment of these debts is likely never to arise. Certainly the number of men who sponsor balanguans is relatively small; furthermore, although debts and ceremonial obligations are in theory inherited matrilineally, especially by a brother, I think these obligations are in fact rarely carried beyond the lifetime of either of the principals. The relationship itself is important and not the debt per se.

been good to him throughout the years—he just comes forth unannounced with a dukduk. The sponsor will think: "Here he is helping me with the real thing" (dowatina). Not everyone is in a position to volunteer in these ways at any given balanguan. For instance, close matrilineal kinsmen of the sponsor, especially the junior members of his apik, will be included automatically in his work group or among his body of supporters. Such a person is already committed, and as a junior member of an apik should not, for instance, make any dramatic effort to enhance his own reputation by volunteering a dukduk. His effort should be limited to such activities as helping his sponsor with divara distribution.

Kinship and Power

The cement casting, the nangwan, the construction arrangements for the dukduks and tubuans—all these define constellations of big men and followers. Kinship expresses these relationships but does not determine them. In my field investigation I asked such questions: Who is helping Doti build his tubuan? Why does Jek spend so much time at Doti's taraiu? Why is Dariut contributing a dukduk to the Doti-Mesak-Koi group? The answers given were the kinship relations I have presented.

An examination of these kinship relationships makes clear that they are of two sorts: some kinship ties impose very strong obligations which must be honored if discredit is to be avoided, and some do not. Dengit, as the true sister's son of the deceased adepts Tomti and Atu, was obligated to be conspicuous in finishing them. But Alipati, who was Dengit's cosponsor, *chose* to be obligated: his relationship to the deceased was not so close as to be inescapable. Rather,

Alipati found—I suspect with little difficulty—an opening in the matamatam so that he could cooperate with his allies Doti and Takaru. If no such convenient opening had existed, or if he had desired a lesser commitment, he could always have volunteered a dukduk.

Most of what is considered kinship is more like the kinship in Alipati's case than that in Dengit's. People usually joined work crews or brought forth dukduks for reasons other than to fulfill kinship obligations. No one is *obligated* to help in a particular balanguan because he is the father's father's mother's alleged sister's son's son of the deceased or of one of the sponsors—anyone can trace this sort of a relationship to anyone else. Instead, big men collect their followers or otherwise unattached men up to the rough numbers actually needed to construct a dukduk or tubuan. These groupings, rather than being a manifestation of a sponsor's genealogical position—such as his seniority and centrality—are a manifestation of his influence.

CHAPTER 7

Construction of the Tubuan and Dukduk

The Power of the Tubuan: the Tubuan Peace and the Kilung Court

The nangwan I have described took place on May 1, 1968. During the following several days construction continued on the dukduks and tubuans. These few days were time enough for the men virtually to complete the tubuans, although work on the physically more elaborate dukduks continued longer. On May 3, a second nangwan feast was held, this time to mark the completion of the tubuan's eyes. Painting the eyes is the critical step in the construction of the tubuan—only minor embellishments such as feather tassels remain to be made—and with the completion of the eyes, the matamatam enters its most important phase.

All aspects of a tubuan's construction with the exception of painting the eyes can be performed by any male who has "seen" the tubuan. Painting the eyes is the prerogative of an adept—the balanguan sponsor himself, who does it in a secluded spot at the edge of the woods adjoining the taraiu. The tubuan figure is only a physical shell, a mask, until the eyes are painted; then it becomes animated: it can see and can, if imprudently treated, kill. When the adept paints the eyes he is bringing back the tubuan's wild and dangerous spirit from its home in the sunset and bringing it under human control.

Immediately with the control of the tubuan's spirit, a period which I term "the tubuan peace" is inaugurated. During this period society appears at its most ordered—at its most domesticated. Everyone is supposed to *ki vakok* (act properly). There is to be no quarreling, no wife-beating, fighting, or shouting. Even little children are not to cry. (What I call the tubuan peace is referred to variously in the Duke of York language as "the time there is a tubuan" or "when everyone ki vakok." There is no economical indigenous term to describe this period.)

By domesticating the tubuan, the Karavarans domesticate themselves. Through ritual with the tubuan they create the image of domestication—or the experience of domestication—and immediately the society is transformed into the actuality of domestication. However, the domestication of the tubuan or of society itself is not always complete. If the tubuan has not been brought and kept fully under control, then it is dangerous, especially to the adept who animated it. During a matamatam there is a series of tests which require the adept to demonstrate publicly that he controls his tubuan. If he cannot control the tubuan it will kill him.

The power of the undomesticated tubuan to kill, it is thought, can be directed as a kind of sorcery. Since no one is ever certain whether or not a tubuan is being used for sorcery—or whether a tubuan is even under proper control—certain precautions which include wearing magically treated red ochre and lime powder are routinely taken any time there is contact with a tubuan, especially one from another community.

If the tubuan is brought under full control, it is still powerful, but its power is used through the kilung court to support order. This court may convene even if a tubuan is not present, in which case it will meet only to enforce the distinctions between ritual grades. If the tubuan is present, as during the tubuan peace, then not only ritual activities but also the entire social field are subject to the tubuan and its court. When an offense against the tubuan peace occurs, the kilung court is immediately assembled. Any male who is permitted to go to the taraiu may be present.

The kilung court is convened—often at night—at the taraiu by the senior ritual adept, the *tene tubuan*. He will state why the court has met in terms so general that it is unclear for some time just who the offender is and what the offense was. Finally the tene tubuan gives the name of the offender and the amount of the fine. Immediately the men begin a chorus of yelping barks, "wukwukwukwuk." After giving the offender a head start to get the divara from his house, the rest of the men follow in a slow procession in complete darkness toward the village, yelping and smashing heavy sticks against trees. Within the village, women and children extinguish their lanterns and huddle in the dark, commenting to each other that the forest has arisen and is invading the village. The expression used is *"bual i kam tur,"* meaning, literally, "the forest stands up." This expression is used at other times when the men invade the village as part of the ritual associated with the tubuan.

Usually the expedition has gone only a short distance into the village when it is met by the offender hurrying back with divara to pay his fine. I was told frequently and in considerable detail that·if this expedition had reached the offender's house before he emerged with his fine, they would have destroyed the house, starting with his treasured corrugated iron roof.

Sometimes the tubuan figure accompanies this group in the collection of the fine. Resistance to the tubuan itself is thought particularly dangerous. There was one Utuan whose legs were badly withered, as a consequence, it was said, of his attacking the tubuan with a knife when it came to his house to collect a fine.[1] There are then compelling reasons for paying the fines. Moreover, I was told that the Australian Administration knew that the tubuan, not the luluai, was in charge during a balanguan and that this arrangement had their full approval. The Administration was regarded as unwilling to interfere with any of the activities of the tubuan. Tomerau, for instance, claimed that there had been cases in which people had gone to the Administration court to claim damages for destruction in response to nonpayment of fines. The court allegedly refused to hear these cases because the tubuan was too strong (dekdek). (Despite Tomerau's claims, we know of no actual instance in which there was recourse to this court.)

When the expedition returns to the taraiu, the fine is placed before the senior adept, the tene tubuan, and only then does discussion of the case begin. Ultimately the senior adept decides whether the fine is justified. Fines are very

---

[1] This man, Tolei, was the closest approximation to a free thinker and a social rebel that we encountered. He had made an incestuous marriage not only within his moiety but to a member of his own liting. He had weathered a series of heavy fines and an enormous amount of public opprobrium. He justified his marriage on the biblical grounds that Eve and her intermarrying matrilineal descendants were clearly not observing moiety prohibitions against incest. Tolei had a good mind and specialized in making complicated dance arrangements.

rarely canceled, although they are sometimes reduced. Once the final amount of the fine is established, it is distributed to all men present, including the offender. These men collectively are the society, symbolized by the tubuan under whose authority the fine was levied. The adepts receive somewhat larger portions than the other men, and receive them first. The matter is then closed.

The power of the tubuan thus is expressed in the activities of the kilung court. This is most dramatically apparent in the collection of the fines.[2] Neither the kilung court nor the tubuan peace which it maintains can, however, be understood in isolation from the vurkurai court and the activities of nonritual life that the vurkurai court maintains and reflects. It is necessary to examine this contrast—a contrast which the Karavarans make explicit—to understand the meaning of the kilung court and the tubuan in providing a statement of those constraints the Karavarans consider necessary if order is to be maintained in their lives. (See Chart 1 for a synopsis of this contrast.)

The Karavarans see the tubuan peace as social life at its most orderly—at its most domesticated. Since many common activities during the tubuan peace are banned, many of the occasions on which quarrels can arise have been eliminated. This also means that any disputes stemming from such

[2] The capacity of the tubuan to impose order is also demonstrated in the concept of balilai. The Karavarans use this term to refer to a variety of instances in which the figure of the tubuan or the adepts impose discipline. In some cases, as when a boy sees the tubuan or dukduk for the first time, he may be struck on the back by adepts and senior males. On other occasions such as the kinivai, host adepts may strike visitors who offer up their backs. Sometimes also the figure of the tubuan may strike volunteers. All of these instances are referred to as balilai.

Chart 1: Contrast between Vurkurai and Kilung courts

Vurkurai	*Kilung*
The offender may refuse to come to the court meeting, there is extensive discussion before the fine, and enforcement is dubious.	The offender is fined first, the case is discussed later, and enforcement is certain.
Cases may be discussed for several meetings of the vurkurai court, and some are never settled.	Cases are always settled immediately.
Fines may be paid in divara or in Australian currency, as specified by the court.	Fines may be paid only in divara.
Rules which are enforced—insofar as they are enforced—are those of everyday interaction. Offenses are between individuals.	Rules enforced cover actions which for the most part are not offenses in everyday life. Offenses are between individuals and the tubuan/community, even when the physical victim is an individual.
The court is not considered to be impartial but rather is regarded as a political forum.	The court is considered to be impartial. It is thought to be the agent of the tubuan and not a political forum.

activities cannot be settled by the tubuan. The kilung court's powers cannot, for instance, be used to enforce the return of bride price in the case of a divorce because divorces cannot be transacted when the tubuan is present. The return of a bride price in case of divorce is a strictly secular matter which must be settled by the usual methods of control through divara and the relative power of the parties involved. Moreover, the vurkurai court is not allowed to convene during the tubuan peace, so even if disputes should arise, they are not allowed public expression.

All fines during the time the tubuan is present, even for an offense such as injuring another person, are paid to the tubuan and its court rather than to the injured party. He, along with the offender, receives merely his share among many when the fine is distributed. Thus the category of offenses against individuals—the basis of the proceedings of the vur-kurai court—has been eliminated: there are only offenses against society.

Most of the offenses brought before the kilung court during this time are not offenses during normal times. A man's beating his wife usually causes little comment: only in exceptional cases, after repeated and extreme violence, will a vur-kurai meet to handle such a case. Quarreling, hitting without drawing blood, and certainly shouting, are everyday events which are not usually considered offenses. Why then does the tubuan enforce conduct which is not required in normal social life?

For the Karavarans, to *ki vakok* (act properly) is to behave in direct opposition to their natural human tendencies, tendencies which expressed themselves fully during the momboto. During normal social life, the time in which the vur-kurai court convenes, the momboto of human nature is allowed expression but is curbed by divara (or cash). By contrast, during the time the tubuan is present and the whole society is subject to its court, even the slightest human tendency toward anarchy is denied expression. Not individuals and their natural greed and violence, but rather the overwhelming power of the tubuan and its kilung court are apparent during the time the tubuan is present. The effect of momboto nature is minimized, while the effect of society is maximized.

Although it was clear to me that much of the activity of the kilung court was dependent upon the influence of big men—ritual adepts—both in the obscure ritual distinctions they were able to cite and in their decisions concerning the amount of the fine, Karavarans considered the court to be impartial because the adepts are regarded only as the agents of the tubuan.[3] Big men themselves are clearly under the tubuan, and, in contrast to the vurkurai court, cases often are brought against big men in the kilung court.

One dramatic case was brought against big men during our field work. Several big men were shouting, fighting, and drunk at the Utuan taraiu later in this matamatam, and they were fined by the Utuan kilung court. The next day one of them, although slightly shamefaced at the drunkenness and fighting, expounded at great length to me that the tubuan is no respecter of particular individuals. It is equally strict, he said, with a child in the village and a big man at the taraiu if either makes a disturbance. He seemed rather proud to have created an opportunity for the power of the tubuan to be demonstrated.

The kilung court and the vurkurai court together encompass in synoptic form social experience for the Karavarans. The vurkurai court, as I have suggested, provides only an incomplete statement about the nature of social order. The order of the vurkurai court—and nonritual life generally—is based on the exercise of power through the me-

[3] The early European accounts of life in New Britain and the Duke of York Islands stressed that the adepts in the dukduk-tubuan society were continually levying fines for trumped-up transgressions, the usual victims being women or uninitiated men (see Rickard 1891:73). Although I doubt that these accounts are entirely accurate—presumably these women had male kinsmen interested in their welfare—they do give the impression that adepts may at that time have had considerably more influence in everyday life than they have now. Salisbury (1966:120) also mentions that among the nearby Tolai an adept may collect fees for adjudicating cases, although Salisbury does not discuss the nature of these cases.

dium of divara. Divara, in this context, is the basis of changing social groupings: big men acquire and lose prestige and followers; kin groups form and reform.

In ritual, as in the matamatam, this kind of political process also is central and in fact is more intense than it is during nonritual life. A matamatam illustrates, par excellence, the exercise of power by individuals. But in addition it constitutes a statement about the limits of the political process and an individual's power. The kilung court, as the court of the tubuan, demonstrates that no one is exempt from the constraints of divara. Even big men are not outside society but are subject to the same constraints of divara as those they impose on their followers. As no one may stand outside society, no one may freely express his antisocial momboto nature. Any form of control other than divara, such as fighting, threats of violence, physical punishment, love magic, or sorcery, is regarded as intrinsically antisocial and characteristic of the momboto. Because a big man can control his followers only through divara and not, for instance, by physical force, his power over them is limited by the medium of power itself—that of divara. Furthermore, because no one is free to operate outside of society, the meaning of divara must be accepted as given and is not therefore subject to redefinition. To redefine the meaning of divara would be to evade its constraints and thus to act as a man of the momboto. Thus divara, in the context of the tubuan peace and the kilung court, has an aspect of permanence, since despite the flux of political contention, the medium—and its meaning—in which this contention is expressed and constrained remains constant. Because the kilung court ensures that divara is the only medium by which men may control each other, it ensures that all power is constrained by the medium of its expression—divara—and that ambition results in social order rather than in anarchy.

The kilung court, then, and the period of the tubuan peace provide answers to the questions raised but left unsolved in the vurkurai court and in everyday life. The question of what it is that limits a big man's power receives its answer: divara, the unalterable medium of that power. The other major question of who are the big men receives its answer: those who control the tubuan. The tubuan peace defines the dominant concerns of the matamatam to be the exercise of power and the limitation of that power. Specific ritual activities during the matamatam that deal with the figure of the tubuan focus more sharply on these same general concerns.

The Second Nangwan

The second nangwan on May 3 which initiated the tubuan peace continued in the theme of the first: it again defined the identity and the autonomy of each of the groups of sponsors. Again four separate nangwans took place at each of the tubuan construction centers, but no combined nangwan occurred at the Doti-Mesak-Koi taraiu. I attended the Doti-Mesak-Koi nangwan and the last portion of the Alipati-Dengit nangwan. At both of these taraius, the tubuans whose eyes had just been painted were displayed on coconut frond mats facing the semicircle of seated diners. At the Doti-Mesak-Koi taraiu, the tubuan was joined by three of the dukduks that were being made there by men who had joined with Doti and the others. The dukduks were still largely incomplete. Although it is usual to display dukduks and tubuans in this fashion for any feast at the taraiu, one reason in this case for displaying the newly completed tubuan was to show that the correct magical formula had been used when

the eyes were painted. Had a mistake been made, the
dullness of the eyes would have revealed that the tubuan was
not animated.

When the men are actually eating, the tubuan is always
turned to face away from them. It is considered to affect the
food in some undefined way. If it is present, an adept passes
lime powder to each man who sniffs it into his nostrils before
eating to keep from becoming bloated. There is no belief,
however, that death would result from omitting this precaution. The dukduks, having no eyes, do not have to be turned
away from those dining.

The first to be served at the Doti taraiu were those who
had worked on the tubuan itself. They were each given a
basket of cooked food with a fathom of divara attached. The
rest of the group were served the same fish and bananas but
were served from a common store. Also present at the Doti-
Mesak-Koi nangwan were all those who were making dukduks for Doti and his cosponsors. Thus, at this nangwan the
sponsors and their allies were clearly distinguished from
those associated with other balanguan centers. No important
speeches followed this nangwan.

I next went to a neighboring taraiu where Dengit and
Alipati presided. Two tubuans were on display there—the
tubuan of Dengit and Alipati and the Pikalambe tubuan
belonging to Lipan and his brothers, mentioned earlier. Here
there were speeches. One was made by Dengit who was almost in tears. He said that this was the taraiu where Atu and
Tomti, the two adepts for whom this balanguan was being
made, used to come and relax; they used to sit at these same
nangwans and now they were dead. This was almost the
only time during the Utuan matamatam that the men, at
least, did seem to mourn the deceased.

The Routine at the Taraiu

Later in the day of May 3, after this second nangwan, a boat chartered primarily by Doti and Alipati left for Rabaul to buy taro at the Rabaul Tolai market, carrying, among others, representatives from each group of sponsors. Doti and Alipati, the two wealthiest sponsors, were good friends and dominant members of their respective groups of sponsors. Both the rental of a boat and the purchase of the taro are usual ceremonial expenses borne by the sponsors. The boat selected was the Kaun, controlled by Ambo of Karavar. The rental fee was twenty dollars, standard for a trip to Rabaul.

At Utuan that night men sat around in their respective taraius with other members of their work group. They sang various dukduk-tubuan songs and some of the young men practiced the dance steps that are used when carrying the dukduk and tubuan. Most evenings during the kumbak were spent this way, with the members of each of the little groups staying together, chatting and singing.

The dukduk and tubuan songs are in Tolai. I inquired why the Duke of York language was not used and was told that it was just insufficient (*pei ot*). Most men speak Tolai quite fluently, since it is very similar to their own language. Furthermore, the United Church Bible is in Tolai and there is a great deal of contact with Tolais through intermarriage, visiting, adoption, and employment in the Rabaul area.

Some of the dukduk-tubuan songs are borrowed from the Tolai; some are the gift of spirits encountered by men of the Duke of York Islands during vigils in the deep bush. At that time they may be visited by bush spirits or ancestors who sometimes give them songs, patterns for new tubuans or dukduks, and magic. The songs often refer to the images from the fasting experience itself. One, for instance, described a man becoming very small and hiding with a tiny bush spirit inside a vine. Although these songs are sung with considerable enjoyment and gusto or just hummed for pleasure, the content is of very little importance. There is no question that they are usually sung without an understanding of the words. Karavarans were surprised when I asked for translations. They were able to translate very haltingly and only when pooling the knowledge of four or five men.

I asked why these songs were sung prior to the actual time when they serve as the dancing music for the tubuan and dukduk. Some said that this was practice so the younger men could learn the songs and thus not be criticized by visitors at a public performance. This concern with the reaction of visitors is a dominant consideration throughout a balanguan. The songs also make the bodies of the men clean and shining and their decorations especially dazzling.

During the daylight hours for the next few days the men continued to work on the dukduks under the direction of their particular sponsoring big man. They worked, slept, and ate together as self-contained groups, each on its own taraiu. Food was provided in large part by the sponsors of the dukduks as well as by the sponsors of the tubuans. Some of these meals consisted of prestige foods, such as rice and tinned meat, that were purchased with cash. A thermos bottle of hot tea was another necessary provision provided by the big man for his workers. Some of the more modest meals were of fish and bananas, prepared by the men themselves at the taraiu. More elaborate meals, especially those involving the fancier baked indigenous foods, were prepared in the village by the women. When such a meal was ready, a whistle was blown—since shouting is prohibited during the tubuan

Plate 3. Thatched ceremonial house at taraiu

peace—and a man went up from the taraiu to the edge of the
village to receive the food. Upon his return to the taraiu, he
washed his feet in the sea to remove any traces of the dust of
the village, which is contaminated by the women. The food
itself, although prepared by the women, does not have the
capacity to contaminate men secluded in the kumbak. Food
customarily passes freely from the village to the taraiu, although not vice versa.

The tubuans, as I have said, were largely complete by the
time of the second nangwan. As a consequence, while the
work on the physically more elaborate dukduks continued,
the sponsors of the tubuans were free to make final practical
and political arrangements for the last phase of the matama-

tam. These included the trip to Rabaul to purchase taro and liquor, and trips to neighboring islands to visit allies in other communities. It was during this period after the tubuans had been completed that the dispute among sponsors, already mentioned, arose over the buturs. I think that Doti's attempt to further his ascendancy, with the ensuing arguments, conferences and adjustments, is typical of this interim period.

The daily routine as I have described it continued, and the work was on schedule. Everyone clearly understood that Wednesday, May 8, was the day that the public and culminating portion of the matamatam would begin. By Monday night only two things remained to be done: the dukduks had yet to be painted—an elaborate procedure that did not take place until Thursday morning, May 9—and a leafy skirt had to be made for each dukduk and tubuan.

Preparation for the collection of the leaves began on Monday evening. Workers fashioned a special kind of palm frond basket about eight feet long to be used in collecting the leaves. The existence of these baskets is secret from the women just as are all the details of the construction of the dukduk or tubuan. The following morning, Tuesday, men from each work camp took the baskets to the large neighboring Duke of York Island, where the requisite leaves (*tangul*) grow. The leaves were gathered and brought back to the Utuan taraius carefully covered in the baskets. The geographical setting was such that this trip could be completed without passing close by any stretch of land where women were likely to be. Women in any event always give the taraiu area a wide berth, both from the land and the sea, and their movements are further curtailed during the ceremonial period. The collection of the leaves was saved until the very end of the construction so that they would appear fresh and green. They were carefully transported in the special baskets lest the salt sea spray dry out the leaves prematurely.

The rest of Tuesday was spent constructing the leaf skirts. The stems of the leaves were fastened together into hoops so that the leaves all hung in one direction. Fastened to the bottom hoop was a pair of vine strap suspenders. To don a dukduk or a tubuan, a man squirms into the bottom hoop, fits the suspenders over his shoulders, and then piles on layers of additional leaf hoops until they reach eye level. On top of all this he holds the head of the dukduk or tubuan securely on his shoulders by means of his uplifted but concealed hands. A number of alterations may be necessary to make the outfit manageable, but invariably a very tight fit results.

Payment of the Women for Cooking

The next day, Wednesday, was the beginning of the public portion of the matamatam. Many women from the adjacent islands of Karavar and Mioko descended on Utuan around 8:00 A.M. and joined the Utuan women already gathered in the village. The women had come on this prearranged day to prepare the fancy dishes that would be given at the balabala presentation several days later in the village. For their labors they were paid in divara. The food itself was provided by the Utuan sponsors and included the taro purchased in Rabaul several days before.

Meanwhile the men of Karavar, Utuan, and Mioko had been assembling at the Utuan taraius. The various sponsors offered betel nut to the more illustrious of the guests. Soon the men put red powder on their right cheeks and white powder on their left cheeks. Powder worn in this way, called *mambat*, has usually been treated by magic to protect the wearer from sorcery. This same red and white powder may be worn, if treated with the proper specific spells, for protection against possible use of the tubuan in sorcery; for protection against magic designed to diminish a man's store of divara while he distributes it; or, if untreated, simply for decoration.

The men began drifting up into the village around 10:00 A.M. Most were looking their best, wearing new waistcloths and carrying newly woven palm frond purses. Both the men and women had dyed their hair black with a commercial dye as they do on any occasion of ceremonial importance. No reason could be given to me for this custom, although with their jet black hair and the red and white powder the men were wearing the colors of the tubuan. I suggested to my best informant that the men intended to look like tubuans but he had obviously never heard of anything that might corroborate my conjecture.

In the village the men seated themselves in the shade at Doti's hamlet. Next, betel nut was passed around to the assembled guests by the younger of the sponsors' followers. The betel nut for these occasions may come from the big man's own trees or he may order one of his followers to provide some. If necessary, betel nut may be purchased from some neighbor for a negligible amount of divara. It is usual—and was the case at Utuan—for men simply to come forward as volunteers and pass out betel nut to the guests. This is an easy and conspicuous means of assisting a sponsor.

The men were gathered to pay the women who were preparing the food. The ban on shouting had been lifted in the village, although not at the taraiu, and there was a great deal of noise. A number of drunk and swaggering men pranced about shouting orders to the women to arrange themselves in rows. Such assertive male behavior is common at any sort of ceremonial occasion, and the same strutting and boasting takes place at the taraiu, where women are of course absent. The women were characteristically rather unresponsive to these commands but in time gradually arranged themselves in rows. Once seated, a number of the sponsors' wives and female kindred walked among them distributing betel nut.

The actual distribution of divara was in the usual ceremonial pattern with the sponsors leading both in physical position and in amount of divara. All the men who had any pretense of being active and responsible members of the community followed. There are several factors which influence the amount of divara contributed. The more important the recipient, the more divara he will receive. The more important the donor, the more he will give. The donor's importance will be shown in a rough way by his position in the line of contributors: those having direct responsibility are in the front of the line and those only helping are in the rear. Except for the very front of the line there is not a strict rank ordering, however. A special tie between donor and recipient also influences the amount of divara given: husbands, for example, may give their wives very large portions.

At the Utuan matamatam, Doti, with a large roll of divara around his neck, led the procession distributing divara to the seated women; he was followed first by the other matamatam sponsors, then by the sponsors of the dukduks. Then came the rest of the Utuans and finally the Karavarans. The Karavarans gave shorter pieces than the others and dropped out earlier. Only a relatively few men, including the sponsors, contributed to each woman. Once started the procession spread out among the women so it was not obvious if certain women were overlooked by any particular donor. A donor

Plate 4. Distribution of divara to women for cooking

would make a special effort to give to his kinswomen, but in his searching about for them he could if he wished easily ignore others and thus conserve his divara.

According to Shelly Errington's data, most women received about the same number of pieces of divara and it is these numbers that they discuss with each other. There are, however, substantial differences in the size of these pieces: the wives of big men, unless they are outstandingly disagreeable, receive larger pieces than the wives of lesser men. The women grumble loudly if they feel the amount given them has not been generous. It may be remembered that when the Karavaran big men were paying for the construction of the cement gravestones, the women who were overlooked in this payment complained loudly and were consequently compensated. The young men who felt themselves short-changed said nothing, although some of them left early. The women commented to Shelly that if the distribution is particularly generous, there is singing and general jubilation among the women. One woman reminisced with great pleasure about a distribution some years earlier on Karavar in which Alipet, as the principal sponsor, exhorted the other men to give generously to the women. He said they should not feel sorry for (mari) their divara but should spend it with abandon. One of the prime attributes of a big man is a reputation for not conserving his divara.

A Meeting of the Kilung Court

Although the distribution of divara to the women concluded the day's scheduled activities, few went home. Most of the visitors stayed in the village itself, where there was no longer any prohibition against making noise, and were entertained in small groups by their Utuan friends. The big men in particular were feted with food and liquor by the Utuan big men. A visiting big man expects generous hospitality from the big men who are his hosts, and failure to receive it is taken either as an intentional insult or as a sign that the host's resources are insufficient. In either case an inadequate reception will be remembered critically. In this hospitality there is a strong current of rivalry and it is not unusual for fights and arguments to break out, especially when the men are drunk. Such a disturbance erupted on this particular day at Utuan.

Before I give an account of this fight and the way it was settled, I should indicate what I suspect was one of the underlying causes. The Karavarans, who were extremely proud that two Americans were living on their island, were afraid that Shelly and I might move to another community. Thus when I quietly went over to Utuan to stay for the kumbak that lasted almost two weeks, the Karavarans became uneasy. On this particular day at Utuan when the women were paid for their cooking, two of the visiting Karavaran big men, Ambo and Tomerau, ordered me to return to Karavar with them that day. I had to refuse, of course, which undoubtedly embarrassed them. They and some of the other Karavarans finally walked away feeling that the Utuans had stolen one of Karavar's Americans. Their resentment may have aggravated the tension always existing on ceremonial occasions, even between allies.

I left Utuan on an errand that day in the late morning. When I returned in midafternoon, a meeting of the kilung court was in session at the taraiu with the Utuan tene tubuan, named Pitai, in charge. By the time I arrived the fines had already been levied and the cases discussed. Apparently the following had taken place: [4] Tomerau, Ambo, and Alipet, the three Karavaran big men, were drinking at the taraiu with a Utuan big man named Otia. Otia was a frequent visitor to Karavar and maintained particularly close ties with

[4] This is the incident referred to earlier in this chapter in the discussion of the tubuan peace and the kilung court.

Tomerau and Ambo. Drinking at the taraiu is quite customary and acceptable; however, Tomerau, Ambo, and Alipet
began to shout and converse very loudly and so violated the
tubuan peace.[5] At about the same time and place another
Karavaran named Kepas began to shout. An adept from
Utuan, Dariut, came running over to quiet the noise and attempted, as an adept, to fine Kepas on the spot. Kepas re-
sisted and tried to strike Dariut; Dariut's actual sister's son,
Papaket, intervened by hitting Kepas. In the several versions
that I heard, all stressed that Dariut and Papaket were close
kinsmen helping each other—although Kepas and Dariut,
too, were in fact members of the same liting.[6]

A number of fines were quickly collected. Kepas received
the heaviest fine, a total of ten fathoms, because he shouted
at the taraiu during the tubuan peace and because he defied
the adept who attempted to fine him. Papaket was fined five
fathoms for shouting and fighting at the taraiu, but his offense was considered less serious than Kepas's since apparently he had been acting in support of the adepts. Alipet,

[5] Noise directly connected with the tubuan and dukduk ritual itself is
always exempt from these rules. Therefore shouting the name of a particular dukduk or tubuan, making the yelping cries when an expedition leaves
the taraiu for the village or for the sea, and orating at the meetings are all
permissible exceptions to the general rule of relative silence.

[6] Kepas was an interesting case of a man who was trying by all means
available to him to become a big man, but for several reasons was not successful. Probably the other big men, such as Alipet, were intentionally
holding back recognition in order to maintain their own positions; however, Kepas continued to try hard—probably too hard—to make the first
rank. He made a number of political mistakes: he purchased the rights to
make a tubuan, but bought them from a kinsman on Mioko, not on Karavar; he arranged the marriage of a junior member of his liting only to
short-change his creditors when he repaid them. Kepas seemed to be continually under strain and was extremely pugnacious when drinking.

Tomerau, and Ambo were together fined a total of ten fathoms for shouting at the taraiu. The fine that was collected from the Utuan, Papaket, was given to Alipet as the senior Karavaran adept and the fines collected from the Karavarans were given to Pitai, the senior Utuan adept. These fines were to be divided later among the Karavaran and the Utuan men, respectively.

After the fines had been transferred into two piles, one in front of Alipet and another in front of Pitai, Mesak, one of the sponsors who was temperamentally a conciliator, made a brief speech calling for a splendid matamatam and for great happiness. Then he made a very typical kind of comment, that the young men should see these fines and be afraid, reiterating the view that the only way to ensure proper behavior is to make individuals afraid to act otherwise. The court broke up after this speech with one Utuan telling Alipet that the Karavarans should not give Kepas anything to drink when next he came to Utuan since he always became disorderly when drunk. In late afternoon Alipet and the other Karavarans left for home amid many cheery farewells.

The following morning when I visited Karavar briefly to pick up some equipment I talked to Tomerau. He seemed resigned to my staying on Utuan in order to complete my work there before returning to Karavar, and was interested in discussing the fines levied upon him and the others the previous day. He was the one who was eager to tell me how the tubuan was no respecter of individuals and would even punish a big man if he had made a disturbance or otherwise violated the tubuan peace.

Evening Activities

After the court had been concluded and most of the Karavarans had returned home, the Utuans lounged about and slept. Finally, late at night in the village, Karavaran and Utuan women sang topical songs. The Karavaran and Utuan women were divided into four groups based on their residence—one group for each half of each island. Often one such group is sponsored by a local big man who will then be primarily responsible for paying them. In such a case a debt will be established between the sponsor of the matamatam and the sponsor of the singers. A big man who wishes to sponsor a group will simply tell the women of his part of the community that he wants them to form a singing group, and they will welcome this opportunity to be given divara. In this particular case at Utuan, no one was sponsoring the Karavaran women; as a consequence only those came who had a special tie to Utuan—women who had been born on Utuan or whose husbands were active in the Utuan matamatam. All the women were paid, although the Karavaran women did not get the bonus that would have been given them if they had had their own sponsor.

The songs themselves, in a mixture of pidgin English and the Duke of York language, cover a great variety of local topics. Some mention recent scandals such as adultery cases; others sadly tell of the departure of a friend. One humorously mocks two women whose canoe capsized, suggesting that they were women of the bush, unaccustomed to the sea. Certainly some of these songs must serve as a rebuke to minor malefactors. Such a song may be composed by anyone—at least any male—although some men have quite a reputation as composers. We have no instance of songs composed by women. Unlike the songs sung when the dukduk or the tubuan dances (*kapilai*) or the songs used in love magic and at funerals (*wurawura*), these topical songs (*gara*) are just thought up and are not acquired through fasting in the forest.

According to Shelly's account, the singing in the village lasted all night. The women sang while walking in a slow procession around the slit gong, which was beaten by one of them.[7] The walk was a slow shuffling dance with occasional bursts of rhythm. During parts of the song they stood still, one foot in front of the other with their right arms flung over and in back of their heads. One woman danced nude—to the great amusement of the others—but since it was dark and no men were present, this was not raw exposure. The predominant attitude was determined hilarity as they forced themselves to sing throughout the entire night. Some women just sat without singing for periods while they rested their sore throats or chatted with their friends. At all times throughout the night at least a few women continued to sing as they trudged through the circular and shuffling dance.

On several occasions during the night—around 9:00 P.M. and then later at 4:00 A.M.—a wave of panic swept the group of singers, who temporarily scattered. In each case there had been a crashing sound that had made the women and chil-

---

[7] The slit gong, or *garamut* as it is called in both pidgin English and the Duke of York language, is a short section of hollowed log about three feet long with a narrow slit opening. The slit gong is played by striking the lip of this slit with a cane pole about an inch in diameter and five or six feet long. Slit gongs have status as quasipersons even though they are not thought to be animated. When broken, one may be included in a mortuary ceremony, as are certain favorite dogs and very large old roosters. They are owned by individuals, generally big men. On Karavar, Alipet and Tonga each owned one. I was told that there should be a feast on the occasion that a slit gong is returned to its owner after it has been on loan: this feast would be at least partly in honor of the slit gong itself. Slit gongs are no longer made in the Duke of York Islands, as the process of hollowing out with fire is laborious as well as technically difficult. No one was able to say whether spells were used in their manufacture. A slit gong is, incidently, a rather nice source of income since the borrower and his supporters will contribute generous lengths of divara for its rental.

dren think a tubuan was coming up through the woods into the village. Although that did not in fact happen during the night, it is common for the dukduks and especially common for the tubuans to patrol the village during the day, scattering the women and children. The main purpose of such an expedition is, in the view of the men, to train the women and children to maintain a respectful distance from these figures. A secondary objective is for the tubuan to look for any men who are in the village rather than at the taraiu where they belong during the matamatam.

While the women could be heard singing in the village, the men were companionably lounging about the little fires at the taraiu as they did every evening during the kumbak. Two young men that night made a systematic tour of all the taraiu work centers. Both had recently paid for the right to see the dukduk, having already seen the secrets of the tubuan. The two young men came to Doti's taraiu, where I was staying, and said they had just paid to see the dukduk. They were escorted into the shelter where Mundiaro's dukduk was residing for the night and given a lantern so that they could see it clearly. After a few minutes they left for the other taraius. These young men, with the exception of myself as an outsider, were the only ones to see all the dukduks before their final unveiling.

Painting the Dukduk

The following morning, Thursday, May 9, all the dukduks were completed, and the kumbak was concluded. The final step in the construction of the dukduk is to apply a special kind of red paint or dye. If the dye sticks properly, the kumbak is considered a success; if the dye is runny, the kumbak is considered a failure. A successful kumbak is one in which men have fully secluded themselves from women; a failure is one in which men have been contaminated through contact with women. The dukduk figure is, then, an indicator of the relations males have had with females during the kumbak. It is also an indicator of the relations males have had with other males during the kumbak. Contact with women is inversely related to male solidarity, a solidarity the Karavarans value because it is one kind of triumph over the divisive inclinations of their momboto nature.

Although most adult males have purchased a dukduk, only the relatively few men who are adepts know the spells necessary for the preparation and application of the red dye. As a consequence, each of the construction groups for both the dukduk and the tubuan was led by an adept or had made arrangements to call on an adept.

I observed the painting of Takaru's dukduk. The preparations began around 11:00 A.M. with Takaru and his full brother Kongkong—both adepts—in charge. They had learned the relevant spells needed in painting the dukduk from their father when they bought the right to make a tubuan from him. Those present at the painting included the original work group, of which Kongkong had been a member, plus a small influx of men who had been making the tubuans. Aping, a Karavaran and a very close classificatory brother of Takaru and Kongkong, belonged to the latter category. He had been helping Doti, Mesak, and Koi with their tubuan during the kumbak, but at this critical period he was present at Takaru's taraiu. While the dukduks were all being painted, the work in the tubuan camps was suspended and most of the men were distributed at the various dukduk construction sites.

As the first preparation, Takaru and Kongkong tied one

end of a long strip of split cane to a tree. Each wrapped a packet of white lime around the cane where it was fastened to the tree and ran with it to the free end, covering the cane with white powder. When I later privately purchased the spells for the construction of the dukduk and the tubuan from Kongkong, I was told that there was no magic used in this lime or in the preparation of the cane strip. If this is true, the lime was probably employed simply because white lime per se has a generalized potency. I was told by a usually well-informed nonadept, however, that this lime had been treated with spells to counteract limited contamination arising from minor violations of the kumbak. A man could be contaminated if he went into the village, especially if he entered a house there.

There is, as shown here, considerable divergence in belief on particulars among both laymen and adepts, although the ideas about the major purpose of an activity are relatively consistent. Thus in the matter of painting the dukduk there may be disagreement about certain features of the procedure, but all were agreed that it was necessary that the rules of the kumbak be observed for the paint to go on properly.

After the split cane was powdered, the palm fronds composing one wall of the shelter where the dukduk had been constructed were removed and the figure was brought out in the open to make it more accessible. It was safe to reveal the dukduk while it was being painted because at this time there was no visiting between the work camps that could result in a contaminated man from another group damaging the dukduk by his presence.

Takaru then walked about the dukduk spraying coconut water from between his teeth. This action had the same purifying effect as the lime used in preparing the cane. I did

collect a spell for the spraying from Kongkong but the meaning is somewhat unclear. It seems to say that the coconut
water should make the paint red and that the magic of other
men—big men who are named specifically—would not be
sufficient to harm the red paint of the dukduk. This spell
then is to prevent sabotage. It is likely, however, that the literal meaning of the spell is not especially significant. Certainly the literal meaning of this and other spells was given to
me in a halting and uncertain manner and did not always
correspond directly with the supposed effect of the spell.

While Takaru sprayed the area with coconut water, everyone else bathed in the sea. The men had to wash off the coconut oil which they customarily rub on themselves and remove any traces of blood—human, fish, or fowl—from their
hands before they made and applied the red paint. It is even
prohibited that a particular kind of insect with a reddish
blood be squashed at this time. One informant said that he
would not scour the red betel nut stains from his teeth until
the dukduk had been painted. If these and the general precautions of the kumbak are not observed, the red paint applied to the dukduk will be runny and not remain confined
within its proper boundaries. (The preparations for painting
the dukduk which I saw on Karavar during 1972 were somewhat more elaborate. At that time several additional steps
were taken to purify the area and the dukduk itself from contamination.)

After the men had bathed, Takaru and Kongkong tied a
strip of the lime-treated cane around the center of the fibrous
cone of the head of the dukduk. This cane, which would
serve as a sort of masking tape, was carefully placed so that
it was strictly horizontal. Then the entire work force began
scraping off the outer skin of a particular kind of root from a

fairly common plant called *mundier* which grows in a variety of places. The bark was scraped with small clam shells freshly collected from the sea. The shell scrapers every man carries in his personal basket to scrape out coconut meat were considered unsuitable because they were contaminated by frequent contact with the village.

From the time that Takaru and Kongkong first began to prepare the cane with the lime there had been intense concentration at the taraiu. The men worked rapidly but carefully. This clearly was serious business and there was no casual chatter. The roots were scraped and the orange scrapings collected and mixed with sea water. Then lime was added, turning the scrapings deep red. The resulting mixture was wrapped a little at a time in the fibrous bast from the coconut tree and squeezed into a leaf receptacle to produce a red dye.[8] It was emphasized to me that this method of squeezing the scrapings to make the red dye was significantly different from the method of preparing coconut cream for domestic consumption. One difference was in the position of the hands. When coconut is prepared, normally by women, though occasionally by men, the cloth-covered packet of scraped coconut is twisted with one hand above the other as in wringing out a wet garment. However, in making the red dye, the hands are parallel and are sawed back and forth. Furthermore, I was told several times what taxing and difficult work making the dye was with perhaps the implication that making the dye is far more arduous than making coconut cream. There was a noticeable huffing and puffing by the men preparing the dye, and, in fact, these labors did appear to be strenuous.

[8] Where the coconut fronds separate from the trunk there is a fiber that looks very much like burlap.

The dye was applied to the dukduk in the circumscribed areas by means of small brushes quickly fabricated from a fibrous wood. A number of men, most of them not adepts, helped to prepare the paint and apply it to the dukduk.

Most of the work in the construction of both the dukduks and the tubuans, as well as in the production of other kinds of ritual paraphernalia, can be done by virtually any male— although some men are recognized as superior craftsmen; the adepts take over only for the relatively few portions of the work requiring spells. Thus in the construction of the tubuan, only the red eyes must be painted by an adept; with the painting of the dukduk, only the purification of the work area must be performed by an adept.

When the painting was almost over on the lower portion of the dukduk, the men relaxed even though there was still a bit more painting to do. For the first time since the task had begun, there were a few quiet jokes and conversation. Even though the job was under control, men were displeased when a canoeist passed by rather far offshore; apparently the dukduk was still vulnerable to contamination. During the entire time only one outside person actually entered this taraiu and that was Doti, who stood at the extreme edge and inquired whether he could enter. He was quickly assured by Takaru that he could, illustrating the difference between an important ally and an insignificant canoeist.

A second red band was painted above the first one on the cone of the dukduk. As before, the cane was carefully wrapped around the cone to create the boundaries of the painted area. The mash of squeezed root scrapings was re-squeezed to produce more dye which was then applied. From a technical point of view Takaru's dukduk must have been quite easy to paint, since its pattern could be easily masked off with cane from the surrounding areas. However, many dukduks have more elaborate patterns on the central cone that require steady freehand work. Finally, the cane was carefully lifted away, leaving sharp boundaries between the painted and the unpainted areas. The dye had not run; there had been no contamination; the kumbak was thus a success. Many of the men immediately took brief naps after this critical work was completed. The waste material from the construction and the dyeing was cleared away and later burned.

During all this time a pot of fish soup had been simmering on the fire at the taraiu. Once the work was concluded the men ate from a common trough. I do not think there was any special significance to this meal except that it represented part of a big man's responsibility to his work force and defined the cooperating group. It was rather typical of the meals served at the taraius during the entire kumbak.

After this respite a post was set up in front of the little shelter that had housed the dukduk on which were arranged the rings of leaves that had been previously assembled for the dukduk's skirt. This arrangement was made with deliberation, and the order of the leafy rings was changed a number of times so that the profile took on just the right contour. Then the freshly painted head of the dukduk was placed on top of all the leafy rings to conclude the arrangements on the post.

As Takaru and his group made these last adjustments, whoops and yelps and the shouted names of the various dukduks being constructed sounded from the other taraius. Such an outcry signified that a particular dukduk was complete. Despite these cries, Takaru's group was not hurried in their arrangements. When finally they had finished, Kongkong went off into the adjacent bush a short distance and emerged

yelping and calling out the name of Takaru's dukduk. The
rest of Takaru's group responded similarly. By this time it
was midafternoon. The completion of the dukduk marked
the completion of the kumbak.

Interpretation of the Meaning of the
Dukduk and Tubuan

The strictures of the kumbak become more intelligible as
the ritual significance of the tubuan and the dukduk is understood:

For a ceremony in which only the tubuan appears, there is
no kumbak. Under these circumstances the men will, to be
sure, spend most of their time at the taraiu, but there are no
prohibitions against visiting the village or having sexual intercourse. There are no such prohibitions even for the adept
whose tubuan is being made and who will utter the spells
that animate it. Furthermore, when the tubuan is made, the
men must prepare and consume the coconut oil called polo;
they are also permitted to eat the coconut sauce, *pokololo*, that
is often an ingredient in baked dishes. Men eat polo, it may
be recalled, to offset the debilitating effects of contact—
especially sexual contact—with women as well as to make
themselves sexually desirable to women. I have suggested
that through polo men acknowledge the sexual desirability of
women but attempt to prevent this desirability from having a
divisive effect on men.

When the dukduk is made, there is always a kumbak, and
for that reason the kumbak is a feature of a matamatam. During the kumbak neither polo nor pokololo, the coconut sauce,
is made or consumed, and contact with women and the village is strictly eschewed. As I have stressed, the men during
the kumbak spend all of their time at the taraiu entirely in

the company of other men except for brief forays after fish, garden produce or construction materials. The kumbak creates for its duration a relatively autonomous all-male society. It is appropriate then that polo, associated as it is with women, is excluded from the kumbak.

The dukduk figure itself is the test of whether or not the kumbak was satisfactorily carried out. If the red dye runs and does not remain confined within its boundaries, it is referred to as *polo* (which literally means "wet"). This means that someone has violated the kumbak by having sexual intercourse during this period and the contamination he brought to the taraiu has ruined the dukduk. (I got only one example of this dye having run. I was told in 1972 that a dukduk Alipet had made the previous year had been a failure. When such an event occurs, the dukduk is destroyed and the whole episode is a source of shame to those concerned.) A man who has had intercourse is also referred to as polo, and I am quite sure that this refers to the wetness of sexual fluids. As one of my informants put it, if a man who has been kumbaking is polo, then the red dye too will be polo. Thus in the kumbak and in the application of the red dye, the condition of being polo must be strictly avoided. In the case of the tubuan there is no kumbak, no sexual abstinence and furthermore, polo is eaten to enhance sexuality. Polo then clearly refers to the sexual relations between men and women.

But what does the redness of the dye mean? If the redness is the redness of blood—no one was able to tell me what this red did represent—then polo (runny) dye would, I suggest, refer to sexual blood, that is, to menstrual blood or the blood of childbirth. Both menstrual blood and the blood of childbirth are regarded as the most concentrated of the pollutants that affect men and as such represent essential femaleness.

Red dye—blood—that was not polo and remained confined would represent the condition of male solidarity symbolized by the "one blood" of the father-son relationship—the model of male solidarity. The successful creation of the dukduk, in contrast to the creation of the tubuan, is the creation by males of another male figure in the complete absence of females and their sexual functions. The kumbak is, I would argue, the transitory representation of an all-male society in which males directly produce males without females.

Through the creation of the dukduk, men show that the reproductive capacity of females can be denied; through the prohibitions of the kumbak against sexual intercourse, men also show that the sexual capacities of women to divide men can be denied. By denying the existence of women, men are able to deny the existence of their own anarchic momboto energy which is often expressed in disputes over women. After a successful kumbak, men feel triumphant because they have achieved a state of male solidarity and order.

But such a state is necessarily without energy and impermanent. Significantly, the dukduk figure is referred to as "only a flower" (*purpur ku*)—a decoration. It is a figure without power or life; it is not animated by a spirit as is the tubuan. Furthermore, the fact that dukduks are made only if tubuans are present (in contrast, a tubuan can be made without dukduks) and that the kumbak is only an interlude in the matamatam is an implicit recognition that a solidary all-male society can exist only in opposition to normal society which includes both men and women. In the kumbak, males define themselves as solidary and reproductively self-sufficient, but only in juxtaposition to women. Society does, in actuality, depend on women to reproduce itself and on the energy of the momboto, which causes humans to act, for its vitality. The dukduk and the kumbak represent a triumph, but an unrealistic and brief one.

In contrast, the dependence of society on women and on momboto nature for its perpetuation and vitality is symbolized in the figure of the tubuan. The tubuan figure expresses both the energy and the control of that energy that are the two essential components of social life. With the domestication of the tubuan, Karavarans domesticate themselves, as shown by the imposed order of the tubuan peace. Since the major concern of the tubuan peace is domestication, it is appropriate that there be at this time a concentration on the greatest obstacle to social order: the activities of women. With the tubuan, female sexuality is not denied, but there is an attempt to mitigate its disruptive effects. This is done in two ways. One is through the use of polo which is consumed whenever a tubuan is made: the capacity of women to divide men is reduced thereby although the sexual desirability of women is not denied. The other way is through emphasizing the capacity of women to bear children.

In a matrilineal society, sexual desirability and childbearing capacity can easily be dissociated since the women whose children strengthen the matrilineal group are not those with whom the men of the group have sexual relations. In the Karavaran context, this distinction is made by defining women as wives or as mothers. I will argue that with the tubuan, there is the attempt to define women through their childbearing capacity—as mothers. This is shown in the kavei when a distinction is made between the women of the tubuan and other women. During the matamatam a similar attempt is made to define women as mothers—in the male efforts to convince the women that the tubuan figure gives birth to the dukduk figures.

The men believe that the women are ignorant of the true nature of the dukduk and the tubuan figures, that is, women do not know that either kind of figure is made by humans. All details of construction and the fact that there is construction at all are carefully kept secret from women. Instead, women are taught that the tubuans, the female figures, give birth to the dukduks, the male figures. The men derive considerable satisfaction from knowing that women are hopelessly confused about ritual matters. Moreover, not only do men wish to hide the truth from women; they wish the women to hold a specific alternative view: they want them to believe that the tubuans give birth to the dukduks.

Two male activities in the matamatam are particularly designed to convey this view to women. On the night before the dukduks are completed—and thus shortly before the women are to see them—the younger men who are helping construct the various dukduks put out after dark in canoes and paddle a few hundred yards off shore. They return shouting out the name of the dukduk on which each has been working. I was told that they intend by this action to tell the women that the dukduks have arrived at the taraiu. The implication is that women are to think that they have suddenly appeared in their completion, as if birth has taken place.

Another minor activity is performed to mislead the women. The tubuan ventures out of the taraiu to the edge of the village with a basket on its arm and collects a kind of green leaf (tumba). It then carries this basket back to the taraiu. Since this green is eaten by mothers to make their milk plentiful, the men intend that the women and children believe that the tubuan is preparing to nurse its young, the dukduks. It is difficult to know just how effective this deception is. Shelly tried to investigate the beliefs held by women about the tubuan and dukduk but she was unable to get women to talk about anything at all concerning them. We thought perhaps the women knew more than they should, and because they were unclear as to just what it was they were supposed to know, they found it prudent not to talk at all. Furthermore, women are not supposed to show an interest in these ritual matters and are probably reluctant to discuss them for fear they will be fined. It is therefore difficult to judge the effectiveness of the male charade. The women do at least act, however, as though they believe the tubuan gives birth to the dukduks, thus accepting the perspective on ritual matters that is given them by the men. The men are, I suggest, attempting to present a model to the women that female sexuality is of an essentially maternal nature.

A partially unresolved question remains about why there are ritual secrets between men and women. Why, specifically, is the way that the tubuan and dukduk are made kept secret from women? The answer lies partly in the fact that men, through their possession of ritual secrets, are able to distinguish themselves from women as those who have power: men have both the vital energy and the energy-controlling divara on which social life is based. Control of the tubuan is both the symbol and the medium of power, a fact evidenced by the adept who controls the tubuan just as he controls society.

Men feel that there are at least some women who actively try to penetrate the secrets of the tubuan and who would make the tubuan if only they knew how. There would be, I think, two possible consequences if women were to make the tubuan. Since women do not control society, their possession of the tubuan could suggest that it no longer symbolized society. As a consequence, the tubuan would be wrenched from its symbolic context. If, however, the tubuan continued to represent society, the implication would be that women wanted to control it so that they could control society. The consequence in this case would be not only disorder but the perversion of order. Women have neither the divara nor the energy on which Karavaran society is seen to rest.

Women could make a tubuan if they knew how; hence, they must be kept in ignorance. Women could not make a dukduk successfully, however, even if they knew how, simply because of their physical nature: they necessarily have intimate contact with menstrual blood and the blood of parturition. The reason for secrecy about the dukduk is, therefore, less clear. Perhaps men fear that if women knew how the dukduk was made they could generalize to the tubuan and thus threaten that secret. Also, if the women knew how the dukduk was created, they would know that the tubuan could not be the mother of the dukduk.

Moreover, for women to accept the view males themselves hold that the tubuan and the dukduk are "unrelated" would not accurately reflect the perspective of women in a matrilineal society. In a matrilineal society, women have no reason to negate the matrilineal tie which is implicit in regarding the tubuan as the mother of the dukduks: for women, their children are their matrikin. Men, however, have a different perspective: for them the patrilateral father-son tie is in many ways preferred to the matrilineal mother's brother–sister's son tie. By regarding the dukduk and the tubuan as fully distinct and unrelated figures, it is possible for men to separate the noncompetitive patrilateral from the competitive matrilineal relations. This separation makes possible the kumbak in which men can act for a while at least as though all of them really did have fundamentally common interests and that coercion and control over others with divara was not an essential part of life. For these reasons, then, men present one view to the women and keep another view secret to themselves.

After the Kumbak

During the kumbak, competition is muted. The crews working on the dukduks are solidary, cooperative units and there is an absence of overt competition between them. Throughout the taraiu, men feel a unity with each other in their seclusion from women. With the conclusion of the kumbak, the matamatam enters another phase. The dukduks come to be associated less with noncompetitive relations; their importance lies more in their role in establishing alliances between big men: they become, in other words, more politicized. Although throughout the conclusion of the matamatam important activities will continue to be held at the taraiu, much of the ceremony takes place in the village in the presence of women and of visiting men. This latter portion of the matamatam is pre-eminently political. Communities compete openly for political standing. Individual big men and their clusters of followers create relations of debt and obligation with each other that reflect and determine the distribution of power. Men as a category interact with women as a category in ways that express the relations of power existing between them. After the conclusion of the kumbak the figure of the tubuan is paramount as both the actual as well as the symbolic medium through which these political relations are established and expressed.

CHAPTER 8

Big Men and the Tubuan

The Tubuans Enter the Village

In the early afternoon, by the time Takaru's group had finished arranging their dukduk for display, the slit gong was already sounding from the village. The men then began rather hastily to apply such personal decorations as fiber armbands with leaf tassels dipped in a mixture of red ochre and coconut oil. None of these had magical or ritual significance; they were worn simply to enhance the wearer's appearance.

By the time I reached the village all four of the tubuans made on Utuan were pacing about. This was their first appearance outside the taraiu and thus their first appearance before the women and children who from then on form an important audience. The entrance of the men and the tubuans is an invasion, as the village is normally considered the women's province, in contrast to the men's domain of the taraiu and the deep forest. During the matamatam when the men leave the taraiu in a group on their way into the village, either in the presence of a tubuan or on business related to the tubuan, they will utter a chorus of yelps and whoops. This signifies that the forest is moving into the village and displacing the women and children. Since women and children are strictly prohibited from approaching the tubuan, and to a lesser degree, the dukduk, they are relegated to the background even in their own village. It is, I think, an effective way of stating that men, by virtue of their control over the tubuan and the associated ritual, are in decisive control over all the activities of society. This invasion is an extension of order from the taraiu into the village commensurate with the imposition of order in the village by the tubuan peace.

During the usual balanguan season, approximately from February to July, or whenever a community in the vicinity has a tubuan, the women are prohibited from conducting any of their own limited ritual activities. For instance, when a bride is escorted to the groom with gifts of food, the women normally sing as a group. They are not even allowed to practice these songs, much less perform them, during the period just mentioned. The total eclipse of women's ritual activities during the tubuan season parallels the physical displacement of women from the village in the presence of the tubuan. This is not to deny, however, that women have positive obligations during a matamatam. One of these, already mentioned, is the cooking of ceremonial food, for which they are paid. Even in participation of this kind, though, women act at the behest of the men and do not direct any part of the matamatam.

When the tubuans at the Utuan matamatam entered the village, certain women wailed. They were wailing at the sight of a tubuan that had either belonged to a particular deceased adept or was made as part of the balanguan that was finishing him. Not only was the tubuan said to remind them of the deceased adept himself but it reminded them of the help in divara that they gave him when he was purchasing it. I have already discussed the process through which a tubuan is purchased and the stake thereby that a man's mother and sisters come to have in it. These are the women—with the addition of his wife—who wail at the sight of his tubuan.

After the tubuans had entered the village and had created their stir there, they were individually escorted to the cemetery. Each sponsor led his own tubuan to the particular graves of the kinsmen he was finishing at the matamatam. Then he broke off one of the ornamental dracaena plants that border the cemetery and escorted his tubuan back to the taraiu where the dracaena was replanted, if space allowed, or was just discarded. The other men of the moiety who were finishing their own kinsmen next were permitted to borrow the tubuan of the particular sponsor with whom they were cooperating in order to visit the cemetery.

My notes are incomplete on this phase of the Utuan matamatam, but Tomerau of Karavar told me what the pattern should be: Tomerau said that the Utuans followed an abbreviated procedure when the tubuans visited the cemetery. (Pejorative comments about other communities usually deal with ritual "unsoundness" and/or stinginess.) Tomerau said the tubuan and its escort should visit the cemeteries on two occasions, instead of just one, as was the case at Utuan. One visit should follow the course observed on Utuan. On another occasion, however, a similar visit should be made to the cemetery by the tubuan with its escort: the dracaena collected at this time would not go to the taraiu but would either be displayed on the butur or presented as a gift.

Tomerau, who was not yet an adept, said that at the forthcoming Karavaran matamatam he would use Alipet's tubuan to visit the cemetery. After each of these trips—there would be as many trips as there were cement gravestones made by Tomerau—Tomerau would pay the tubuan carrier, any strong young man of Alipet's apik, with a half fathom of divara tied up in a package with betel nut. In addition, Tomerau would tie divara to the stalks of dracaena just collected and give them to selected individuals of the opposite moiety. Thus if Tomerau, a Pikalambe, were to return from visiting the gravestone of an important mother's brother, he would tie five fathoms to the dracaena and give it to a Maramar. If Tomerau had visited the grave of a child or an insignificant man, then only one fathom would be tied to the dracaena. The recipient of this divara would return payment to Tomerau when the recipient and his moiety made a balanguan. This is still another opportunity, then, in the course of a balanguan to establish alliances through debt and anticipated repayment.

At the Utuan matamatam, after the individual tubuans had visited the cemetery and carried the dracaena down to the taraiu, each returned independently to the village. In the village, at the command of its sponsor, the tubuan knelt and men, women, and children of the apik of the sponsor approached and threw down little leaf packets in front of it. The men came directly up to the tubuan but the women and children rather gingerly tossed their packets from a distance. These packets contained not only betel nut and the peppers customarily eaten with it, but also short lengths of divara. A similar presentation has been mentioned before: when the dukduk that Nemeya was transferring to his sons came to Karavar, such packets were given to it. Unlike the presentation to the dukduk, all the gifts to the tubuan during the matamatam were unmarked, since presentations to the tubuan are not repaid. It should be remembered, however, that because these packets are presented in person, the fact that a gift was brought is noticed, even though the particular packet and its contents may be anonymous.

Not only packets of betel nut and divara but also in some cases personal property of the deceased were brought forward. The personal items were generally of little value but were intimately associated with the deceased, such as an old army jacket, a hat, and a cane. All of these relics would be placed on the butur the following day. The collection was gathered into a basket and carried by the tubuan's sponsor as he and the tubuan left for the taraiu. There the divara was strung into a continuous length, as it usually is after a distribution, and it, plus the betel nut, accrued to the sponsor.

The Kinivai

The next morning, Friday, May 10, preparations for the kinivai began. On a kinivai the men of an entire community, irrespective of distinctions such as moiety or apik membership, travel with a tubuan in a canoe flotilla to a matamatam on a neighboring island. Before I had seen a balanguan, the parts that were most often described to me were the kumbak and the kinivai. The men greatly enjoy the kinivai and reminisce in detail about their own kinivais, favorably contrasting them with those performed by other communities.

A kinivai is often sponsored by a big man of the participating community who is responsible for leading in the payment of those who have gone on the kinivai. The sponsor of the kinivai thereby opens a debt with one of the sponsors of the matamatam that will be repaid in kind with a kinivai when the former gives a matamatam. During the kinivai the members of a community put themselves on display as a distinct social group under the direction of a big man and under the aegis of a tubuan. As they land on the shores of their matamatam hosts, they are met in mock battle by their hosts and the host's tubuans. The boundary between the host community and the guests is very clearly drawn. Society in its most restricted geographical sense as the local community is defined through this encounter. The tubuan is essential in the symbolization of society on the level of the local community.

On Karavar there was a great deal of activity on Thursday evening and again on Friday morning preparing for the kinivai to Utuan. Alipet and Tonga, the two senior Karavaran adepts, supervised. On Thursday night the men sang dukduk and tubuan songs (*kapilai*) late into the night while they prepared and consumed polo, an activity, it may be remembered, associated with the tubuan and not with the dukduk. If the kinivai has a sponsor, the polo will be made from his coconuts. Since there was no sponsor in this kinivai to Utuan, the polo came from coconuts grown on the small plot of communal land adjacent to the Karavaran taraiu.

Alipet and Tonga mixed several kinds of ointments and powders. Tonga made an ointment called *wurtop* (or *langoran*) which is a mixture of red ochre, coconut oil, crushed flowers and a nutlike kernel. The men rubbed this ointment all over their bodies to make them feel light and invigorated, so they could dance and sing ecstatically. Tonga was considered to have very superior magic for making wurtop; this accounted, the Karavarans claimed, for their magnificent dance performances that allegedly made them the envy of the Duke of Yorks.[1] The same preparation, as well as polo, is used for a liu to make the men dance so that the women will desire them.

---

[1] Tonga taught the spell for making *wurtop* to Kepas, and Kepas taught it to me after Tonga's death. Kepas explained that Tonga had taught him because Atu, Kepas's father, and Tonga cooperated in ceremonial matters and thus considered themselves to be brothers. A kinship relationship of father and son was later established between Tonga and Kepas because Kepas spent a lot of time in Tonga's company. Finally Kepas asked him

While this was going on, the other men prepared ornaments such as feather clusters for their hair and tassels of leaves to be worn around the forehead and arms. Usually the men also make special baskets. These are like the purses of woven coconut fronds carried by every adult male except that for the kinivai they are made larger and with long tassels to which fresh greenery is attached. For the kinivai to Utuan, the baskets were not made, an omission which provoked censure from the Utuan hosts.

The explicit purpose of the wurtop, the polo and the decorations is so to impress the hosts with the splendid appearance and singing of the visitors that the hosts will dance on the beach with excitement and joy as the kinivai approaches. Clearly, however, this joy may turn to envy, provoking the hosts to attempt to destroy the kinivai through sorcery. Others, too, may work sorcery on the kinivai. To protect against such dangers, Tonga and Alipet each made further preparations: Tonga made the spells for the lime and the red ochre that the men would wear on the kinivai. These white and red powders (*mambat*) are worn on the cheeks on visits to any community where there is a tubuan. Alipet also magically

---

for this spell and Tonga agreed to teach him. There was no charge for it nor is there a charge for any spells except those which comprise part of the formal purchase of the tubuan.

The spell for the wurtop can be translated roughly as a command for the wurtop to shake the faces of the dancers and the village dancing ground; for all to gather round and watch the man who has given the spell; to make his drum and dancing tremble; for all to shout and whoop. The general meaning is clear, although Kepas was not able fully to explain all the references. He excused himself by saying that this spell originated from a fast in the woods and thus contained images that were intelligible only to the person having the vision. Practically all the spells we collected are, like this one, a series of direct commands, but the agent to carry out these commands is not clearly specified.

treated lime which would be thrown to protect the Karavarans when the kinivai arrived at the Utuan beach.

Early Friday morning two Utuan tubuans went to Karavar. One was the Pikalambe tubuan made by Lipan; the
other was a Maramar tubuan made by Alipati-Dengit to finish Atu and Tomti. When the two tubuans arrived on Karavar, the tubuan made by Alipati-Dengit went immediately to
the house of Kepas, Atu's son. There Kepas gave the tubuan
a number of the personal belongings he had inherited from
his father. The tubuan then left for Utuan immediately,
without ceremony, and carried Atu's relics to the butur that
was under construction in Dengit's hamlet.

A kinivai requires a tubuan. No Karavaran had been asked
or had volunteered to contribute a tubuan, either as an ally
or a cosponsor, to the Utuan matamatam. Therefore, the
Lipan tubuan, a Pikalambe tubuan, was loaned to them for
the kinivai. It went directly to the Karavaran taraiu where it
remained until it left with the kinivai. Although the Karavarans who went on the kinivai included members of both
moieties, they were going as visitors to a Maramar matamatam. Since the important activities that day would include
the establishment of ties between Piklambe guests and Maramar hosts, in a large measure the entire interaction between
guests and hosts was viewed as between Pikalambes and
Maramars. Thus it was appropriate for the Karavaran guests
to be escorted by a Pikalambe tubuan. Another reason for
selecting that particular tubuan may have been that the rest
of the tubuans would be engaged in other activities on Utuan
prior to the arrival of the Karavarans. As Lipan was not a
sponsor, his tubuan could be loaned out without curtailing
any activities central to the matamatam.

Around midmorning on Utuan, when word came that the

Plate 5. Tubuan and canoes offshore on the kinivai

kinivai was approaching, all the men still in the village joined the rest at the taraiu. The Mioko kinivai landed before the Karavaran kinivai and disembarked at the Doti-Mesak-Koi taraiu. This taraiu was chosen because the link for this occasion between Mioko and Utuan was through Koi and Mundiaro. Koi was from Mioko and Mundiaro, who was co-operating in this balanguan with his Mioko kin, had built his dukduk at this taraiu. Mundiaro's kin had built two tubuans on Mioko which were used for the Mioko kinivai.

The Karavaran landing came only a few minutes later. As the Karavarans approached they were visible for a long distance to those watching from the Alipati-Dengit taraiu. This taraiu had been selected for the landing because on this occasion the Karavaran connection with Utuan was through Atu, one of those for whom Alipati and Dengit were sponsoring the balanguan. Atu was considered a Karavaran, although his closest matrikin were from Utuan. When the Karavaran flotilla was within about fifty yards of this taraiu it paused offshore while the men seated in their canoes sang and drummed with renewed frenzy and the escorting tubuan danced in the lead canoe.

Meanwhile, all the men gathered on the beach, including the new arrivals just in from Mioko. A group of adepts were prancing about by the edge of the water in welcome. They were doing the dance (*malamala*) reserved for adepts in which the adept hops on one foot with the other leg bent at the knee, all the while waving a spear. The level of noise, the expenditure of energy, and the feeling of excitement were overwhelming. After a few minutes the Karavarans moved in and landed. As the first of them beached their canoes, the Utuan tubuans that had been concealed in the background charged

Plate 6. Karavarans landing on Utuan at conclusion of the kinivai

across the beach at the Karavaran visitors. They were accompanied by yet another group of adepts carrying spears. White lime was thrown by the adepts leading the charge of tubuans down to the water's edge. The Karavarans responded by throwing their own lime as they ran from their canoes into the Utuan attack. Then many of the Karavarans stopped meekly in front of the host adepts to receive a blow across the back with a palm frond core.[2] Suddenly all the whooping and shouting stopped; the participants staggered about leaning on each other for support as they caught their breath. Once the men had recovered a bit they shook hands, some bathed in the sea, and all collected themselves.

There is throughout the entire balanguan, but most emphatically during the kinivai, a strong element of competition and distrust between local groups that underlies the expressions of hospitality by the hosts to their guests. The preparation for the kinivai itself reflects this competition and distrust: The men apply mambat as defense against sorcery, and the spells for the mambat specifically name prominent members of the host groups so that their attempts to use a tubuan—or other means—to sorcerize the guests will be unsuccessful. The lime powder that is thrown on the arrival at the beach by both hosts and guests is treated with magic. If the magic of each side is of equal strength, nothing will happen, but if there is a discrepancy between them, the man carrying the tubuan of the weaker side will suffer a misfortune humiliating to his community. This encounter was described to me as a contest between magics.

This sort of sorcery is expected and sharpens the juxtaposition between hosts and guests. In contrast, there is a

[2] This too is called *balilai*, the general term used when men submit to the power and discipline of the tubuan.

pointlessly destructive sorcery, thought to be worked by a solitary man watching the kinivai from a distance. Such an individual would appear to be a social outcast, neither a host nor guest in the kinivai. The belief in this sorcery is a recognition, I think, of the fate which sometimes overtakes a big man. I mentioned earlier the case of Tonga, a former big man who no longer could actively influence political affairs after the expenditure of his divara but who was still feared for his knowledge of magic. Tonga, in the bitterness of his relative social impotence, sometimes did attack out of spite the exercise of those privileges he had himself once enjoyed as a big man and is the sort of person who might be suspected of trying to destroy the kinivai.

Still another source of danger to the kinivai derives from the opportunity it presents for women to penetrate the tubuan secrets. The kinivai with its dancing tubuan is visible to the women as it travels by sea from one taraiu to another. Women are thought to use an unspecified kind of sorcery on the passing tubuan so that it will come apart and thus reveal what is inside. If women were to see the tubuan come apart and learn the details of its internal construction, they would of course still have to learn the spells necessary to install and control the spirit of the tubuan before they could actually make one. They would, however, have penetrated the first line of male defense.

The object of much of this sorcery, that expected both from the hosts and from either male or female bystanders, is to make the man carrying the tubuan stumble and fall so that he will let go of the top portion of the tubuan or to make him swell and burst out of his already very snug costume. In the sorcery performed by men, this is to happen at the taraiu; when performed by women, in a public place.

The sorcery is directed against the carrier, not against the tubuan spirit itself, which by virtue of its own power is invulnerable. For this sorcery to be effective, the names of the carriers must be known; they are, consequently, kept secret and the carriers are given a special kind of mambat (protective decoration) in addition to the standard mambat worn by all the men.

The Village Dancing Ground and the Introduction of the Dukduks and Tubuans

After the canoes from the kinivai had been beached and the men had rested briefly from their exertions, hosts and visitors alike adjourned to the village. That morning the buturs had been constructed in the village. Just as the nangwan feasts had defined each group of sponsors by specifying their location at the taraiu, the buturs defined each group of sponsors by specifying their location in the village. Each group of sponsors constructed a butur in its home hamlet. There were three buturs on Utuan—in the hamlet of Dengit, of Doti, and of Bangut. The home hamlet of the fourth group of sponsors was on Mioko: since all the ceremonial activities were on Utuan, I suspect they did not build a butor.

At the buturs great rolls or circles of divara were displayed, along with relics from the various deceased being finished in this matamatam, including those belonging to Atu brought by the tubuan from Karavar early that morning. Circles of divara are called *kuar;* they contain approximately one hundred to six hundred fathoms of divara spliced into a continuous length which are then carefully arranged into circles and wrapped with split cane. The final product resembles a new tire, still in its factory wrapping. The amount of divara in a kuar is not standard although always a multiple of ten.

Divara is wrapped up this way for several reasons, the most important being, I think, that it is considered an impressive sight. It is thought, also, to be relatively safe in this form from certain kinds of sorcery that cause divara to disappear. And of course a man is less tempted to fritter away divara if it is done up in a kuar.

Bystanders estimated for me the amount of divara at Dengit and Alipati's butur at about four thousand fathoms.[3] Some had been brought by Alipati himself; most of the rest was provided by Alipati and Dengit's Maramar kin. Since this was a Maramar balanguan, there was no rental paid for their display. I do know that the only kuar at Doti's butur to receive a rental fee belonged to a Pikalambe, Pitai, who was also making a dukduk for Doti.

The first set of speeches when the men had reassembled in the village following the kinivai were at the Dengit-Alipati butur. Alipati welcomed the guests to what he called a very small insignificant balanguan. This self depreciation was belied by the butur beside him on which substantial circles of divara were displayed. The speeches of the big men frequently show either a false modesty or blatant boasting about the importance of the speaker. Such bragging—in either form—is expected and, to judge from the early accounts (Danks n.d.:4), entirely traditional.

Following the brief oration by Alipati, the men moved off

---

[3] Unlike the Tolai balanguans described by Epstein (1969) and Salisbury (1966) the large amounts of divara placed on display in these kuars are *not* broken open and distributed. As a consequence, the Duke of York mortuary ceremonies involve much smaller expenditures of divara than do the Tolai balanguans.

to Doti's hamlet several hundred yards away. The rolls of divara and the relics were transported from Dengit and Alipati's butur and added to those already at Doti's. The same procedure was followed by the other sponsors on Utuan. Just as was the case with the first nangwan feast, initial recognition was given to the separate standing of the several groups of sponsors, but the Doti-Mesak-Koi group was shown to be of paramount importance.

Doti's hamlet remained the center for subsequent activities: The men gathered in a large circle in the foreground and the women and children settled themselves discreetly to the rear. The center was kept clear as an arena; just to the side of the arena were the butur and the slit gong. For the next several hours the tubuan and dukduk figures were escorted sin-

Plate 7. Doti's butur, dancing ground, and slit gong

Plate 8. Tubuan in the village

Plate 9. Greeting a dukduk with lime powder in the village

gly into Doti's hamlet and officially greeted, as it were, by the adepts there. As tubuan or dukduk approached, accompanied by its owner and his supporters, the slit gong sounded a continuing beat and the host adepts danced about with spears. Once it entered the arena, the adepts charged, spears held as though ready to be thrown. One of these spearmen would throw a package of lime that would puff up like smoke. In response, lime would be thrown by the owner-escort of the figure as it had shortly before at the beach when the kinivai landed. After the figure had been introduced in this manner, it danced for a few minutes and then retired from the dancing ground to the taraiu.

A dancing ground is not just any level open piece of ground. Each dancing ground should have a *palivat*, that is, a stand of ornamental dracaena plants with a stone buried beneath. As part of the procedure at his first balanguan, an adept constructs a palivat at his taraiu and at his hamlet dance ground. Then he steps onto the ground above the buried stone to steady himself so that he will not be distracted by the crowd and so that he and his ceremony will be imposing (*mawat*).

The palivat is also thought to act as a sort of magnet for any magic left about after the tubuan dances. When the tubuan dances and bounces around, there is the danger that some of the lime powder from its face and red paint from its eyes will fall on the ground. They are so highly charged with magic that women and children coming in contact with them would become sick. The palivat in the village and in the taraiu should protect women and children by attracting the dangerous elements, although it is not itself dangerous and children can, for instance, play on a village palivat.

After all of the tubuans and dukduks had been greeted at the dancing ground, they regrouped at the Utuan taraiu and returned together to the village in a single file, led by a column of all the visiting adepts. The first row of adepts carried palm fronds that partly obscured those who followed; in back of them were the other adepts, then the tubuans, and finally, the dukduks. The slit gong in the village gave the rhythm, and the whole line advanced in a two-step called a *nowo*. The host adepts advanced from the village in this same two-step toward the procession emerging from the woods. As the two groups drew close, the host adepts charged with spears at the guest adepts, the tubuans and dukduks. Again lime was thrown in great puffs. This confrontation between hosts and guests, which was omitted at the two other matamatams that I witnessed, was similar to the ones that took place at the kinivai and on the village dancing ground a short time before.

Striking the Tubuan

The next event, the *tutupur*, is a confrontation, not between hosts and guests but between adepts and their own tubuans. I have suggested that a matamatam is concerned with succession, the replacement of the deceased big men by living big men. The matamatam provides a series of tests and, in some cases, ordeals, that require a sponsor to prove publicly that he is a big man.

If the tubuan is the master symbol which stands for society itself, then a man who controls the tubuan is a big man for he shows he can control society. This is the reason that big men must be adepts. The sponsor of the matamatam must successfully survive a series of ordeals that test his control of the tubuan. The first, as we have seen, entails successfully painting the tubuan's eyes. The next and most decisive encounter is the tutupur, when the adept strikes the tubuan with a roll of divara. If he does not utter the proper spell the tubuan will kill him. If the sponsor survives the encounter, it demonstrates very explicitly that he is indeed a big man: he is one who controls the tubuan/society with divara. The final ordeal comes when the tubuan is deactivated. At this time its spirit is released and returns to its home in the sunset. If the tubuan had been made for "insufficient reason"—if the balanguan has not been adequate—then the spirit will linger and cause the death of the adept who originally installed it in the figure of the tubuan.

In a less abstract way a matamatam sponsor proves that he is a big man by ordering the behavior of others through divara: when he shows that he has a following, he demonstrates his ability to impose order within his own community. In addition, he engages in exchanges of divara with established big men. Although big men are not able to control each other as fully as a big man controls his followers, they create alliances through their exchanges that do, to a limited extent, order their political relations between their respective communities. Big men show in the matamatam that they can impose order not only within their own community but also between communities.

The remainder of the matamatam is then an intensive demonstration of who it is that can act as a big man.

For the Utuan tutupur, the tubuans and dukduks which had just arrived at the dancing ground from the taraiu were arranged in a semicircle. The tubuans were lined up together adjacent to the dukduks. Each figure knelt on the ground and small packets of betel nut were thrown down in front of some of them. Then the owner of each figure came forward and laid one to two fathoms of divara in front of it. Next, a member of each of the four sponsoring groups came forward together and each faced his own tubuan. In unison each stamped the ground with the left foot, reared backwards

Plate 10. Tubuans and dukduks kneeling for the tutupur

rather like a baseball pitcher and threw a roll of ten fathoms of divara into the leafy body of his kneeling tubuan. Each of the dukduks was similarly struck. These men were adepts; striking the figures is one of their prerogatives. Tutupur—striking of the tubuan with divara—has some of the characteristics of an assault, and magic must be used to protect against the tubuan's retaliation. The adepts protect themselves by uttering a spell just before throwing the divara. Because it is of the utmost importance that the protective spell be efficacious, it should be learned from someone trustworthy.[4] (See Chapter 4 for a discussion of the problems in selecting a trustworthy teacher.)

[4] I collected two versions of the spell for the *tutupur*. One consists simply in uttering the name of a powerful bush spirit, *Pupuongen*. I know of no

Plate 11. Tutupur

After the tubuans and the dukduks have all been struck, the owners gather up the divara, consisting of the initial length of between one and two fathoms plus the ten fathom length with which each was struck. The divara is then handed to the tubuan or dukduk figure who carries it off to the taraiu. The shorter length always accrues as payment to the man who carried the figure. Usually the carrier is a young follower of the sponsor of the dukduk or tubuan.

---

particular connection between Pupuongen and the tubuan. The other spell refers to the tubuan as very impressive but says that the man uttering the spell is impressive also. The divara with which the tubuan will be struck is described as belonging both to the tubuan and to its owner. There is a request that this divara expended return to the owner in his future activities.

Sometimes, however, he is loaned to the sponsor by another big man with the expectation that this loan will be reciprocated later. The ten fathom length goes to pay the work force of the figure's sponsor.

The Exchanges

After the tutupur was concluded and the dukduks and tubuans had returned to the taraiu, the distribution of divara, which would last the next several hours, began in the village. This distribution was of critical importance in shaping and reflecting political relations. First Doti called for all visiting adepts to line up to receive pieces of divara from all of the Utuan adepts in recognition of their mutual status. The pieces of divara that I saw given were about eight inches to a foot long and the length of these pieces was to become a *cause célèbre* in the next few weeks.

The controversy stemming from this presentation again illustrates the competition latent in all the activities of the balanguan. For instance, despite the appearance of wild enthusiasm of the hosts at the approach of a kinivai, there are fears of sorcery caused by jealousy. Similarly, visiting big men are given liquor and prestigious tinned food by their hosts in immoderate amounts, but this generosity aims to impress the guests with the wealth of the host and to forestall any future criticism. Guests are indeed quick to note, as they were at this presentation on Utuan, whether the hospitality is in any way deficient.

Although the presentation to the visiting adepts had been made only by the Utuans, both the Utuans and Karavarans were accused several days later by their rivals of being men of no substance. The Miokons and their allies said that the Utuans and Karavarans had no right to swagger around as big men do, boasting and shouting "I, I"—short for "I am a man of divara, I am"—since they were unable to give the adepts pieces of divara longer than a little finger. Relations between the two political blocks became particularly strained and a few weeks after the matamatam, Karavarans and Utuans met together on Karavar to discuss strategy.

At the meeting Alipet of Karavar inquired whether any of the men could describe the ritual of the *anga na pindik*. No one knew much about it but it was supposed to involve a display of enormous amounts of divara that would forever silence the aspersions of the Mioko faction. Although nothing came of the plan to stage an anga na pindik, the prospect of it boosted Karavaran-Utuan morale. (George Brown, the early Methodist missionary, reported [1910:92–93] that he saw this anga na pindik ceremony in the 1880's, but even at that time it was archaic and largely forgotten.)

After the visiting adepts at the Utuan matamatam were given divara as a group, more selective exchanges began. They were of two principal types: The first is called *namatan*, which means "to look in the face." During the namatan, individuals circulate, giving small pieces of divara to anyone they choose. These gifts are to be repaid at the next matamatam at which both donor and recipient are present. Anyone can participate in the namatan irrespective of importance, moiety affiliation, or position as host or guest. In this regard, the namatan differs significantly from the more important exchanges, called *balabala*, which follow it. The balabala, which means "to return," or "to exchange," much more than the namatan, establishes formal political relations.

During the first and most important of the balabala presentations, the sponsors, each followed by his supporters, seek out other big men with whom they wish to initiate an exchange. The sponsor begins the presentation by dropping a large piece of divara in front of the recipient, and his followers contribute smaller pieces. Later, lesser men lead smaller processions to recipients of their choice. Usually the presentation of divara accompanies a gift from the leader, consisting perhaps of the indigenous food prepared earlier for this presentation by the women, or of European food or of some relic taken from the butur.

When Tomerau was helping me to understand the exchanges that took place during the Utuan balabala, he immediately got out a basket which contained small bundles of divara, and a notebook in which he had made entries. Tomerau knew which group had given him which bundle of divara and in most cases he remembered the particular individual in a group who had contributed each separate piece. In his notebook Tomerau had recorded the name of the leader, the nature of the gift, and the total amount of divara received from the group. His list covered these entries:

Alipati	bag of rice	4 fathoms
Kepas		3 fathoms
Tomerikan	2 tins of meat, tomap and tapioca	4 fathoms
Twembe	cup	1 fathom
Bangut	a decorative sprig	a number of small pieces
Tanglik	cup	1½ fathoms

The bag of rice was the 56-pound size costing about $A5.00; tomap and tapioca were both cooked balabala feast dishes; the cups were relics from the butur; the decorative sprig was also from the butur.

The most important of these presentations was the one from Alipati. From the Karavaran point of view, the three most important men participating at the Utuan matamatam were Doti, Takaru, and Alipati. Each of these three had agreed to select one of the three Karavaran big men— Tomerau, Ambo, and Alipet—as exchange partners. A debt was established between Tomerau and Alipati, Ambo and Doti, and Alipet and Takaru. Tomerau, as the least secure of the Karavaran big men, was, I know, pleased indeed to have been selected in this manner. One of the reasons that these Karavarans were selected by the Utuans was that they were known to be planning a balanguan, at which time they would repay these debts. The effect of this partnership was immediately apparent. Both Doti and Takaru demonstrated interest in the balanguan of their allies by visiting Karavar during the construction of the gravestones (see Chapter 5). Furthermore, Alipet asked Takaru to cooperate when a group of men purchased the tubuan from him.

The most politically significant presentations of the balabala are made by an apik. Apiks become particularly important in ceremonial contexts since they provide a big man with the followers necessary to make impressive presentations. In fact, as I have mentioned, an apik is defined by the Karavarans as a group of litings pulled together by a big man's divara to make balanguans. The more followers a big man has at the balanguan exchanges, the more prestige he will have, both because of the sheer number of followers and because of the amounts of divara that can be presented. Since the obligations created by the exchange are only between the big man who led the procession of contributors and the recipient, it is only the leader who will be repaid at a later date by the recipient. Yet most of the divara in the presentation was contributed by people other than the leader himself.

Some of this divara exchanged between big men may, however, filter back to the followers. Such a minor redistribution is possible because these presentations are not repaid in full. The recipient must return only two-thirds to three-fourths of the amount of divara he received, leaving a small profit that can be shared with the followers. Tomerau shared only one of the six presentations he had received: he gave his liting (Tomerau does not yet control an apik) the presentation from Tomerikan which consisted of tinned meat, several kinds of cooked food, and four fathoms of divara. When it is Tomerau's turn to pay Tomerikan back, his followers will collectively return to Tomerau the exact kind and amount of food but only three of the original four fathoms received from him. Tomerau will then repay Tomerikan with this amount. Thus Tomerau's liting will make a small profit of one fathom and will have had a share in the transaction. From Tomerau's point of view, he has transferred some of the obligation of repayment to the members of his liting. He has taken full responsibility, however, for returning all the other presentations. All the food, including the rice, will have to be repaid in exact kind and amount; a relic from the butur will be returned if one was received; [5] the divara will be returned less the small profit kept by Tomerau, and in one case, by his liting.

In contrast, Alipet redistributed to his followers much more of the divara presented to him and hence he shared

[5] A person has first call to use the relics of his close relatives in his own exchanges. Once they are distributed, however, he has no further claim on them. The dead truly are "finished" with this dispersal of their most personal possessions.

more of the profit than did Tomerau. These followers, who are members of his apik (which, incidentally, on ceremonial occasions subsumes part of Tomerau's liting), will accompany Alipet when he makes the repayments and each will return only a portion of the divara which Alipet earlier gave him from the original presentation.

Occasionally a follower, with permission of his big man, may lead the procession to someone of his own choice. In such a case the big man as well as the other followers will contribute to this presentation. When the repayment occurs, this temporary leader will be paid back and will thus get a return well in excess of his own contribution. In actual fact, however, such a reversal of normal leadership is infrequent.

Not all of the exchanges initiated in the balabala were between fully established big men: some were between lesser men or between men of unequal status. There are several ways that a man without an extensive following can enter into such exchanges and increase his prestige. As I just mentioned, a follower can on occasion briefly lead the apik of which he is a member. Furthermore he may have to operate as a member of an apik only during the first part of the balabala when the top-level transactions between the established big men are taking place; after this he may be able to gain control of his own liting and remove them temporarily from the apik. Since women participate as followers in the balabala exchanges, almost any reasonably senior male can at least briefly have the support of some of the women of his liting.

It is therefore possible for men to initiate exchanges with others somewhat more important than themselves. If the aspiring big man conducts himself in these exchanges in an assertive and generous fashion, and if an exchange creates bonds which spill over into nonritual cooperation that is satisfactory to both, the prestige of the lesser man may be enhanced. The full confirmation of his prestige would come if his exchange partner called on him for ritual assistance, perhaps in making a dukduk at a balanguan.

In all of the dukduk and tubuan rituals, and particularly in the matamatam, big men from separate local communities interact. The relationships that they establish with each other reflect and determine to a very great extent the relationships that exist and will exist between their respective communities. These may be of open competition, alliance, or something in between. Of the kinds of relationships, alliance is the most difficult to establish and the most fragile; relationships of competition occur simply in the absence of relationships of alliance. A matamatam provides a series of opportunities for establishing alliances through exchange. The final portion of the matamatam with the namatan and the balabala is only an intensification of the same emphasis on establishing alliances that was present in the earlier stages of the matamatam.

At this point in the Utuan matamatam the public presentations of divara on which much of the meaning of the matamatam rests were complete. The following summary is of those presentations which took place during the final, rather than the preparatory, portion of the matamatam:

nangwan	sponsors pay for some of the feast food
balabala	sponsors followed by all other males pay all the women present for having cooked food
wamama	the tubuans, and later the dukduks, are given gifts which include divara by men, women, and children of the apik or liting of the man who

	sponsored the construction of a particular tubuan or dukduk
no indig- enous term	sponsors of the matamatam lead in payment of divara to visiting adepts
tutupur	sponsors strike tubuans and dukduks with divara which goes to pay men in the work crews who constructed them
namatan	informal distribution of divara from anyone to anyone on an individual basis; no formal obligation for repayment
balabala	formal presentation of divara primarily from the sponsors of the matamatam to other big men, often visitors of the opposite moiety; formal obligation of repayment

The final presentations at the Utuan matamatam I have just described took place in very heavy rain.[6] The dancing of the tubuans and the dukduks which was to follow was accordingly put off until the next day, Saturday.

The Conclusion of the Matamatam

On Saturday, May 11, I returned to Utuan in midmorning, in advance of the other Karavarans who were to follow in the afternoon. Takaru had chosen this time to take a collection for his dukduk. At some point during the course of the matamatam all the tubuans and dukduks are given packets containing betel nut and pieces of divara. The tubuans

[6] There was, incidentally, a good deal of speculation as to why it had rained. Some thought Doti had magically induced the rain so the ceremony would be cut short and he could thereby conserve his divara; others suggested that unknown enemies of Doti sought to spoil the glorious occasion by bringing on the rain.

had received theirs several days earlier. Takaru's dukduk came up from the taraiu to his hamlet, knelt, and was given the packets, which were then carried off to the taraiu. All of the proceeds belonged to Takaru. The divara totaled fourteen fathoms, of which he gave one-half fathom to the carrier in return for his service. A bit later the dukduk ventured forth again into the village. This time it carried a basket containing an empty tin can and a bottle, indicating that it wished to be given food and liquor, to be consumed by Takaru and his supporters at the taraiu. The meager response proved there was nothing coercive about its requests.

During the early afternoon the slit gong sounded in the village and the Utuans again assembled at the dancing ground in Doti's hamlet, which had been the center of activities for the entire matamatam. The tubuans and dukduks appeared singly or in groups and performed their rather stereotyped dance. In midafternoon the Karavarans arrived in the village as a group, although they had not traveled in a flotilla. They had not been ceremonially greeted at the taraiu as they had been earlier with the kinivai, but they were treated with deference and the more important of them were seated immediately in the front row of the singing and drumming men. Shortly after 4:00 P.M. the dancing and singing stopped and the dukduks, tubuans, and men left the village to gather again at the Doti-Mesak-Koi taraiu.

Once at the taraiu the men seated themselves in a semicircle facing a row of the dukduk and tubuan masks which had just been shed by the carriers. Then the tubuan spirits were dispatched. Koi, as the senior sponsor of the matamatam, came forward and muttered an explanation of why the tubuans had been made. He was explaining to the deceased Maramar adepts who were associated in life with this partic-

Plate 12. Tubuans dancing to male chorus

ular taraiu that the tubuans had been made for a serious purpose—as part of the balanguan—and that these deceased adepts should permit the spirits of the tubuans to depart. Then Koi picked up a betel nut from the pile of feast food and threw it over the heads of the men into the woods. With this, the spirits of the tubuan departed from the masks and returned to the sunset where they would remain until needed to animate other tubuan masks.[7] As he threw this betel nut, a group of young men who had been crouching in the woods at the edge of the taraiu dashed forward. Each grabbed a dukduk or a tubuan mask by the top, pushed it from one side

[7] I could find out nothing about the nature of the spirit when it is in the sunset.

to the other and then, swinging the conical masks around their heads, retreated to the woods. This treatment of the tubuans and dukduks is called *pupulung*, a term that also refers to wringing a chicken's neck. It seems to demonstrate that the tubuan's spirit has in fact been released because the masks are now harmless and can be treated aggressively without danger.

At the present time there are only two situations in which the deceased ancestors engage the living. One is the fast in the deep forest. The other is the case just described, when the deceased adepts are invoked, often by name, and asked to release the spirit of the tubuan. If the tubuan had been created and animated for insufficient reason, then the spirit would not be allowed to depart. It would instead linger in the taraiu and in the village, constituting a special danger to the owner of the tubuan and visiting upon him a wasting illness and death. No medicine—neither indigenous nor European—is thought sufficient to reverse the course of such an illness. The logic here appears to be that if a man sponsors a tubuan but does not carry the balanguan through satisfactorily, or perhaps does not even make a balanguan at all, he fails to prove himself a big man and therefore fails fully to control the tubuan.

Following the pupulung the food was passed out to the seated men and lime powder was carried around to be sniffed into the nostrils. The powder had been magically treated to offset the fact that the tubuans had faced the food. If this precaution had not been observed, the diners would have become bloated. Apparently such prophylactic measures are inadequate for the man who dispatches the tubuans and his food is therefore kept hidden from them. The food eaten at this feast had been purchased by the sponsors and prepared by their wives and female matrikin.

The usual round of speeches followed the feast. Alipati said that he, Doti, and Mesak no longer were ashamed but now were free of their mortuary obligations. Various of the Maramar matamatam principals then spoke, thanking the Pikalambes for their help. Mesak, in addition, said that it was a fine thing that Mioko, Utuan, and Karavar had cooperated so splendidly. Amid these protestations of good will and rejoicing, however, there were several criticisms of specific events in the matamatam. Koi, speaking as a Miokon, criticized the way both Utuans and Karavarans applied the red and white face powders (*mambat*). In the Karavaran-Utuan custom, red powder was applied to the right cheek and white to the left. Koi said that such a pattern was a prerogative of the adepts, and the nonadepts should have only white on the forehead. Koi was not only criticizing Utuans and Karavarans for not conforming to the Mioko pattern, he was attempting to make even more explicit the distinctions between adepts and nonadepts. Moreover, he was saying, in effect, that the nonadepts, by wearing only the white forehead band of lime, should be decorated like the women. Koi's view on this matter was later ignored by Karavarans and Utuans partly because of its Miokon origin. His views, though, illustrate a common kind of jealousy regarding ritual prerogatives. (Many cases in the kilung courts concern the usurpation of prerogatives belonging to a higher ritual grade.) Doti concluded the evening with a brief comment criticizing the Karavarans because they had not made special baskets to carry with them on the kinivai. With this the group dispersed.

Two days later, on Monday, May 13, the final, rather anticlimactic episode of the matamatam occurred. The Karavarans did not attend *en masse*, although a fair number came individually. The matamatam as a whole had the purpose of escorting the dead out of society; the final portion of the matamatam provided the same service for the tubuans and the dukduks. Although the spirits of the tubuans had already been dispatched during the pupulung several days before, on this last day of the matamatam the tubuans and dukduks again appeared. Because the tubuan masks were no longer animated the men did not apply protective decoration but instead smudged their faces with black as a sign of mourning for the dead tubuans. The tubuans and dukduks walked slowly along the central path that joins the various Utuan hamlets led by the Doti-Mesak-Koi tubuan, which was limping and walked with a cane. The other dukduks and tubuans straggled along behind, each pretending to brush flies from its companions as though they were already dead. (The term for this funereal procession is *lu lang*, which means to shoo away flies.) In the background women wailed in mourning. As they passed the dancing ground in Doti's hamlet, the slit gong sounded a dirgelike roll and the figures did a few listless bounces which contrasted sharply with the former vigor of their dancing. The procession turned off the path at the cemetery and went directly to the Doti-Mesak-Koi taraiu.

There the tubuans were immediately taken into the woods and dismantled. The feathers were saved for later occasions, but the other remains of the tubuans were thrown into a special area to decay, a portion of the bush still within the boundaries of the general taraiu area. This area is so dangerous that no one goes directly onto it and the remains of tubuans are simply tossed into it from a distance.[8]

In contrast, the dukduks were dismantled casually at the taraiu and their remains later burned without ceremony, as

[8] The association here of decay and danger seems similar to the association Douglas (1966) makes between disintegration and power.

had been the scraps left about after the dukduk construction. They were burned, not because they were dangerous and had to be destroyed, but because the taraiu would otherwise be cluttered. The alternative would be to throw the refuse into the sea, but if this were done there was always a chance that some of it would be washed ashore and seen by the women, who might guess that the dukduks and tubuans were made by humans and did not just suddenly appear fully formed. The fact that the dukduks were discarded just as were other kinds of trash at the taraiu, while the tubuans were considered dangerous even after their spirits had departed, is consistent with the way these two figures are regarded. The tubuan as an eternal and dangerous power must at all times be treated circumspectly; the dukduk is never powerful and is important for short periods only.

The meal that followed the procession of the moribund dukduks and tubuans in the village and their subsequent dismantling at the taraiu is called *gul*, a term that refers to a particular dish primarily composed of taro. Sometimes a sponsor may have his tubuan linger for several weeks after the other dukduks and tubuans have been dismantled, although such was not the case at the Utuan matamatam. Such a sponsor will then provide his own gul after the gul for the other figures has already taken place. The sponsor who withholds his tubuan derives prestige from the extra expense of providing a delayed feast.

The speeches following the gul were similar to those two days before at the pupulung. Again the sponsors said how happy they were to be free of obligation. In addition, a prominent Pikalambe said that this matamatam had been an inspiration to all of them. This was interpreted by some to mean that he was himself making preparations to sponsor a matamatam. A Karavaran then said that, unlike the women and children on Karavar, the women and children on Utuan were not sufficiently afraid of the tubuan and crowded too close to it. An Utuan criticized the young men who had carried the tubuans and dukduks while they were drunk. There had been the danger, he said, that they might slip and fall, that their dances might not be well executed and that the women might laugh at them.

Thus the matamatam for which active preparations had begun at least some four years earlier eased to an end.

CHAPTER 9

Conclusion

I have been primarily concerned with understanding the implicit logic of Karavaran society, most specifically the Karavaran concepts of the nature and basis of order. Order, in their view, can be achieved only with difficulty. Order—social form—is created through the constraint of man's anarchic momboto nature by divara (shell money) in the context of moiety. Power, the imposition of order through divara, is exercised by big men—those who control others in their society. The crucial questions in Karavaran life concern the identity of those who exercise power and the limitations of their power. Who, then, are those who constrain the anarchic momboto nature of others and what is it that constrains those who constrain others? These questions as well as the Karavaran answers to them are implicit in the juxtaposition of nonritual with ritual life.

Karavaran nonritual life is concerned with the exercise of power and the flux of social process. Ritual life is concerned with the constraints of power and the boundaries of social relationships. Ritual thus completes the Karavarans' image of their social reality. Not only does ritual help the Karavarans make sense of their world, it answers practical questions about how people are to live together. Questions of meaning are practical questions for the Karavarans because they lack a concept of structure. In the absence of fixed reference points such as those provided by structure, someone is defined only through the way he participates in a relationship of juxtaposition.

Karavaran society is big men in action. A big man exists as a big man only through his activities of imposing order—it is impossible to define a big man except operationally. The consequence, then, is that the meaning of being a big man comes only in his activity through which he is juxtaposed with his followers and with other big men. Meaning comes through social activity: epistemological problems are practical problems. The locus of meaning is the same as the locus of order.

In the absence of a concept of structure the practical problem of how there can be social order—how individuals can be domesticated—is solved only through the activities of big men. It therefore becomes of crucial importance to know who the big men are and what they do. It also becomes crucial to know what the limits are on their activities. Ritual provides the occasion for men to prove that they are big men. Because society in action *is* the activity of big men, ritual, too, must be society in action if it is to provide the opportunity for men to act as big men.

Ritual is society in action—but in a concentrated and highly ordered form. With the domestication of the tubuan, the tubuan peace is immediately created. In this period the Karavarans appear at their most domesticated: everyone, including the big men, is constrained by the power of the tubuan as manifested in the kilung court. The tubuan peace is not an image or a blueprint of an ordered society; it is ordered society. Within the basic context of the order of the tubuan peace, order is further and explicitly extended to delineate the form of specific relationships.

Much of the dukduk and tubuan ritual specifies and creates

the relationship between men and women, between men of the same moiety, and between men of opposite moieties. The solidarity of males during the kumbak is expressed by their seclusion from, and juxtaposition with, women while they are constructing the dukduk: there is a feeling of male triumph at the successful completion of the kumbak because they have been able to live in concord with each other, in relations untainted by disruptive momboto nature. This harmony is seen as following the model of the father-son relationship. A different image of males, both in their relations to each other and to women, is presented with the tubuan. The nature of these relationships is expressed in the preparation and consumption of polo, and in relations big men have with each other and with their followers. The kumbak with the dukduk, and the tubuan peace with the tubuan specify through juxtaposition two different ways that men may interact with women and two different ways that men may interact with each other. The structure of the matamatam as a whole indicates that those relations between males and between males and females represented and established with the tubuan are the relations on which society during its nonritual phase is based. These statements during ritual define the boundaries—the limits—of the relationships that compose nonritual life.

Karavaran life can be understood only if the Karavaran system of meaning and beliefs is understood. It would be impossible to make satisfactory sense of the reason that the Karavarans juxtapose the vurkurai and the kilung court or the reason that a matamatam sponsor strikes the tubuan with divara without knowing what big men, divara, and the tubuan mean. Big men, divara, and the tubuan are not "brute data" which exist apart from and which can be understood without reference to their meaning for the actors (Taylor 1971). Big men, divara, the tubuan *are* what they mean to the Karavarans.

In the introduction I cited Geertz and Taylor, who provide compelling substantiation for the position I am advocating, namely that the beliefs members of a society hold about themselves constitute their social reality, and, hence, to understand that reality, it is necessary to understand their own beliefs about themselves—their system of meaning. Geertz (1973:6) illustrates this position by comparing a wink and a twitch. From the point of view of the outsider they are indistinguishable contractions of an eyelid. "Yet the difference, however unphotographable, between a twitch and a wink is vast; as anyone unfortunate enough to have had the first taken for the second knows." If we want to understand twitches and winks—or anything else that a member of society does—it is the meaning of that action that constitutes its reality. To cite Geertz again: "As Ryle points out, the winker has not done two things, contracted his eyelids and winked, while the twitcher has done only one, contracted his eyelids. Contracting your eyelids on purpose when there exists a public code in which so doing counts as a conspiratorial signal *is* winking." Taylor, makes this same point by using the example of voting (1971:25–26): No amount of raising hands or marking and counting pieces of paper can be considered voting unless there is the significance—the meaning—attached to this behavior that an autonomous choice is being made such that some decision or verdict is delivered.

If, then, big men, divara, and the tubuan *are* what big men, divara, and the tubuan mean to the Karavarans, some important implications follow. Anthropologists have traditionally examined and interpreted tribal societies in terms of social structure: status, role, norm, office, and so on. There are two classic anthropological perspectives on social structure. One is that social structure is real and that beliefs held by the members of a society about their own society constitute a kind of "false consciousness" which conceals the underlying reality of social structure (see Fortes and Evans-Pritchard 1964:18–21). The other perspective is that the social structure of the anthropological analysis at least approximates the beliefs held by members of a society about their own society. In this view, a group actually sees, for example, the relationship between mother's brother–sister's son as a bundle of rights and obligations—norms—which define their respective statuses (see Radcliffe-Brown 1965). What the anthropologist does is to ferret out these beliefs and arrange them together in a tidy pattern.

My response to the first of these anthropological perspectives is—as I have just argued—that the beliefs of a society about itself are the reality that must be understood. A society is unintelligible to the anthropologist unless it is understood in terms of its own logic. My response to the second perspective is that whether or not there exist societies which do think of themselves in social structural terms, the Karavarans do not.

To interpret in terms of social structure a society such as Karavar—and I suspect that there are many of this sort—which does not understand itself in the logic of social structural analysis is to distort its inner logic and thus make it largely unintelligible. Anthropological social structural analysis is not adequate in cases of this sort. It is essential, then, to learn to think in nonstructural terms—to become permeable to indigenous concepts of social order which may be very different from those concepts in which anthropologists have been accustomed to think.

I have tried in this book to understand the logic of Karavaran society in other than social structural terms. In so doing, a number of fruitful questions have emerged. If the Karavarans do not, for instance, think of social order as resting on structure—either social structure or personal character structure—on what is order predicated? By examining the Karavaran data in light of this kind of question, major aspects of Karavaran life become understandable.

I have been arguing that meaning is inherent in and not apart from activity: meaning resides in social form, not apart from it. Symbols, as well, should not be regarded as standing apart from the symbolized.[1] One of the conclusions that arises from my analysis of Karavaran social life from this perspective concerns the nature of symbols. How is it that symbols—and hence ritual—have effect?

I have already stated that the matamatam is not a blueprint or a model of society in action—rather, it *is* society in action. To put it in a different way, the ritual is not just a statement of order, it is an ordering. At the moment that the tubuan is domesticated, society itself is domesticated: the tubuan peace is the immediate consequence of the adept's controlling the tubuan spirit.

Through domesticating the tubuan, Karavarans domesticate themselves. The tubuan does not just symbolize a big man's control of others; it is the medium by which a big man controls others. Just as the tubuan is the symbol and the means of social order, polo is both the symbol and the means

[1] I am using the term "symbol" in a way different from its usual meaning of that which stands for or represents something else.

of ordered male/female interaction. The dukduk is both the symbol and the means of male solidarity. In all of these cases, the symbol does not stand apart from what it symbolizes. It is effective because it can only be understood in action. The symbol thus creates that which it depicts.

The Karavarans have no abstract political theory; they are not able to present analytic interpretation of their ritual figures or of other aspects of the ritual. A possible reason for this lack lies in the nature of symbols and meaning. I have suggested that the symbol does not stand apart from what it symbolizes; I have argued that meaning in general lies in operation: that is, a big man means "one who controls others with divara." I was puzzled during my early research by the way the Karavarans would speak about the "meaning" (*kukeraina*) of the tubuan.[2] One way in which they would talk about the purchase of the tubuan was to speak of "buying the meaning" of the tubuan; adepts are defined as those who "know the meaning of the tubuan." I expected that as I learned the secrets of the tubuan, a cosmology would be revealed to me in which at least quasi-philosophical statements would be made about the abstract meaning of the tubuan. Eventually, I learned that the "meaning" of the tubuan is the *set of operations* through which the tubuan is constructed and a social relationship established with it. These operations include the spells by which the tubuan spirit is brought under control and installed in the eyes of the tubuan figure as well as other spells—such as for the tutupur—that are necessary for the control of the tubuan. The way in which the Karavarans themselves speak of the "meaning" of

[2] I translate *kukeraina* as the English word "meaning" because if we asked what the *kukeraina* of a Karavaran word was we would be given a Karavaran synonym or an example of its usage in a phrase.

the tubuan is thus consistent with the interpretation of ritual efficacy and the nature of symbols that I am presenting.

Ritual and symbol communicate to the Karavarans something about their society. But the communication is in the form of social action. The meaning of society—or social order—can only be expressed through an ordering. The Karavarans do not have "empty rituals" or "meaningless forms" because meaning and action cannot be separated. The consequence is that because epistemological concerns are practical concerns, social life by its very nature is invested with meaning.

Glossary

apik	Members of the same moiety who are the kinsmen/followers of a big man
balabala	The major exchange in a matamatam
balilai	Submission to the authority and discipline of the tubuan
butur	Ceremonial stand during a mortuary ceremony on which are displayed divara and personal possessions of the deceased
divara	Shell money
dukduk	"Male" ritual figure
go kalei	Reimbursement of shell money spent for a boy at the time he first visits the men's ground
gul	Final meal at a mortuary ceremony
inambua	Vigil in the deep forest to receive inspiration from spirits
kambina tubuan	Tubuan pattern purchased by adept at conclusion of his training
Kaun	A cargoistic business enterprise
kavei	Ceremony in which new adepts purchase with shell money rights to make the tubuan
kilung	Fine levied for ritual transgressions; or a court which meets to levy such a fine
kinivai	Ceremonial movement between communities by canoe in the company of a tubuan
kuar	A large roll or circle of shell money
kumbak	Seclusion of men at the men's ground
liting	A small matrilineal group, the members of which consider themselves to be closely related
liu	One kind of mortuary ceremony in which no tubuan is constructed

lokor	Deep forest
luluai	Government-appointed village headman
malamala	Hopping dance, normally performed only by ritual adepts
mambat	Magically treated protective decoration
Maramar	The name of one of the moieties
mari	To have compassion
matamatam	Major mortuary ceremony for which both dukduks and tubuans are constructed
momboto	The "dark ages" prior to the arrival of missionaries: a period of anarchy conceptualized as the inversion of present society; or, the anarchic energy underlying human behavior
namatan	One of the presentations of divara at a matamatam in which anyone can give to anyone else
nangwan	A feast at the beginning of the matamatam
naur	A man who spends too much time in the company of women
Pikalambe	The name of one of the moieties
palivat	A ritually treated area that protects the uninitiated from contact with the tubuan and which is a source of strength for a ceremonial sponsor
palom	A large quantity of food that is given to a boy when he buys the dukduk
polo	A coconut oil preparation drunk by the men to preserve their health; also has the general meaning of "wet" or "runny"
pupulung	The occasion in which the tubuan is killed and its spirit is released
tagan	A small basket containing European items that is part of the payment when a boy buys the dukduk
taraiu	Men's ground in general, as well as the subdivisions within it which are associated with particular litings
tene tubuan	The senior and most important ritual adepts of a community

tubuan	"Female" ritual figure; also a term applied to the senior and most important ritual adepts of a community
turangan	Bush spirit
tutupur	The ritual striking of a tubuan or dukduk with shell money
vanai	Novice in the process of being initiated into a ritual grade
varvangala	Patrilateral descendants of a man
vavina na tubuan	A woman who has helped a male matrikinsman purchase a tubuan
wamama	A presentation of betel nut, often accompanied by shell money
waturpat	Inauguration of an adept and his tubuan
wurtop	A magically treated ointment to aid a dancer in his performance

Calendar of Events at
the Utuan Matamatam

Late April	Kumbak begins
May 1	First nangwan
May 2	Work on dukduks and tubuans continues
May 3	Second nangwan; sponsors go to Rabaul to buy taro and other supplies
May 4–6	Work on dukduks continues; tubuans largely completed
May 7	Leaf skirts made for both dukduks and tubuans
May 8	Public portion of matamatam begins; payment to women for cooking
May 9	Dukduks are painted and kumbak is thus concluded; tubuans enter village for first time, visit cemetery and are given betel nut and divara
May 10	Kinivai; formal introduction of dukduks and tubuans in village; namatan and balabala presentations
May 11	Tubuans and dukduks dance; tubuan's spirit released; feast at taraiu
May 12	Men rest because it is Sunday
May 13	Dukduks and tubuans walk through village as though already dead; dukduks and tubuans dismantled at taraiu; final feast of matamatam

Bibliography

Aristotle. 1961. *Politics*. Trans. by Ernest Barker. London: Oxford University Press.

Berndt, Ronald. 1965. "The Kamano, Usurufa, Jate and Fore of the Eastern Highlands." In P. Lawrence and M. Meggitt, ed., *Gods, Ghosts and Men in Melanesia*. Melbourne: Oxford University Press.

Brown, George. 1910. *Melanesians and Polynesians*. London: MacMillan.

Danks, Benjamin. n.d. "Burial Customs, Mythology, and After Life in New Britain and Duke of York Island." Mitchell Library Collection, Sydney.

Douglas, Mary. 1966. *Purity and Danger*. London: Routledge & Kegan Paul.

Epstein, A. L. 1968. "Power, Politics and Leadership: Some Central African and Melanesian Contrasts." In M. Swartz, ed., *Local-Level Politics*, Chicago: Aldine.

——. 1969. *Matupit: Land, Politics, and Change among the Tolai of New Britain*. Canberra: Australian National University Press.

Epstein, T. S. 1968. *Capitalism, Primitive and Modern: Some Aspects of Tolai Economic Growth*. Canberra: Australian National University Press.

Errington, Frederick. 1974. "Indigenous Ideas of Order, Time and Transition in a New Guinea Cargo Movement." *American Ethnologist* 1 (2):255–268.

Fortes, M., and Evans-Pritchard, E. E. 1964. "Introduction." Fortes and Evans-Pritchard, eds., *African Political Systems*. London: Oxford University Press.

Geertz, Clifford. 1964. "Ideology as a Cultural System." In D. Apter, ed., *Ideology and Discontent*. London: Free Press of Glencoe.

———. 1973. "Thick Description: Toward an Interpretive Theory of Culture." In *The Interpretation of Cultures*. New York: Basic Books.

Hogbin, Ian. 1970. *The Island of Menstruating Men*. Scranton: Chandler.

Kirsch, Thomas. 1969. "Loose Structure: Theory or Description." In H.-D. Evers, ed., *Loosely Structured Social Systems: Thailand in Comparative Perspective*. New Haven: Yale University Southeast Asia Studies.

Oliver, Douglas. 1955. *A Solomon Island Society*. Boston: Beacon.

Parkinson, Richard. 1907. *Thirty Years in the Southseas*. Trans. from the German by N. C. Barry. In collection of Australian National University Library, Canberra.

Pospisil, L. 1958. *Kapauku Papuans and Their Law*. Yale University Publications in Anthropology, No. 54. New Haven.

Radcliffe-Brown, A. R. 1965. "On Social Structure." In *Structure and Function in Primitive Society*. New York: The Free Press.

Read, K. E. 1955. "Morality and the Concept of Person among the Gahuku-Gama." *Oceania* 25 (4):233–82.

Rickard, R. H. 1891. "The Dukduk Association of New Britain." Royal Society of Victoria, *Proceedings*, 1890, 3 (n.s.):46–52.

Salisbury, Richard. 1966. "Politics and Shell-money Finance in New Britain." In M. Swartz, V. Turner, A. Tuden, eds., *Political Anthropology*. Chicago: Aldine.

———. 1970a. "Dukduks, Dualism and Descent Groups: the Place of Parkinson in Ethnological Theory." An unpublished paper presented at the Bismarcks Conference in Santa Cruz, California, June 1970.

———. 1970b. *Vunamami*. Berkeley: University of California Press.

Taylor, Charles. 1971. "Interpretation and the Sciences of Man." *Review of Metaphysics* 25 (1):3–51.

Turner, Victor. 1967. "Mukanda: The Rite of Circumcision." In *The Forest of Symbols*. Ithaca: Cornell University Press.

Index

Administration, 56n, 67, 142, 169
Adoption, 43–45; between ritual sponsors, 146; in determining mortuary obligations, 44, 159–160; in purchase of the dukduk, 92–98
Anti-council movement, see Kaun
Anti-society, see Momboto
Apik, definition of, 36–38; process of formation, 46–48
Aristotle, 73–74

Big man, 15, 24–29, 48, 243–246, 248–249; assertion of own advantage in ritual by, 97; changing rules by, 73–74; control of the tubuan by, 118, 203, 224–226; decline of power of, 150–151, 217; defining characteristics of, 38, 46, 99, 117, 123–124, 141, 167, 185, 219, 224–225; limits of power of, 66, 74–75, 173–175; relations with followers of, 35–43, 68–72, 132, 163–165, 231–233; relations with other big men of, 49, 96, 128, 130–131, 135–136, 144–145, 154–162, 180, 185–186, 189, 210, 225, 228–231, 234–235
Blood, 50, 61, 194, 199–200, 204
Brideprice, 39–42, 47, 51, 59, 120, 171
Brown, George, 21, 229

Cannibalism, 21
Cargo movement, see Kaun
Character, absence of, 25–29, 66, 248
Circumcision, 61n
Community solidarity, 113, 126, 133, 141–142, 210–212, 216
Councils, see Local Government Councils
Court, indigenous: contrast between each type of, 6, 66, 75, 170–173; kilung, 75, 81–82, 168–175, 186–188, 244; vurkurai, 66–75

Dead, 177, 238; as ritual adepts, 236–238; finished at matamatam, 99, 122, 134, 232n; gravestones made for, 126–131; mourning for, 48, 176, 207, 240
Divara, 22–30, 58, 137–139, 218–219; as constraint of power, 75, 81, 174–175; control of tubuan by, 224–227; control of women by, 119–121; ritual presentation of, 83, 105–107, 131–133, 182–185, 228–235
Dreams, 13 1n
Dukduk, 31, 249; contrast with tubuan of, 91, 98, 102–104, 107, 110–111, 151, 154–155, 204–205, 209, 241; learning secrets of, 90, 191; made by, 102, 154, 163; meaning of, 101, 199–201, 204–205; painting of, 191–197; purchase of, 91–110

Epistemology, 27, 243–244, 256
Epstein, A. L., 17, 24, 219
Epstein, T. S., 17
Errington, Shelly, 32, 50, 60, 83, 184–186, 190, 203
Europeans and Americans, 22–23, 69, 186, 238
Evans-Pritchard, E. E., 247

Feasting, 86–87, 105–106, 128, 131, 139–140, 145–148, 175–176, 238, 241
Fortes, Meyer, 247
Funerals, 38–39, 41, 53–54, 136

Gardens, 16, 40–41, 69, 139
Geertz, Clifford, 19, 246
Genealogies, 36–38, 42–45, 53–54, 152–159, 165

Homosexual behavior in ritual, 84
Human nature, concept of, see Momboto

Incest, 21, 64, 169n
Inheritance, 52–56

Kaun, 125n, 138, 142, 148
Kinship, 23, 25, 35–37, 42–43, 48–49, 56,
    129, 164–165; terms of, 36; *see also*
    Apik, Big man, Liting, Matrilineality,
    Moiety, *and* Patrilaterality
Kirsch, Thomas, 24

Liting, definition of, 37
Local Government Councils, 146
Luluai 67, 129, 148, 169

Male solidarity, 59–60, 64–65, 102, 108,
    199–200, 205, 245; *see also* Seclusion of
    males
Marriage, 39–40, 100, 104
Matamatam, 98–99, 113, 122–126, 245;
    outline of events of, 142–144; reasons
    for giving of, 98–101
Matrilineality, 25, 29, 35–49; contrast with
    patrilaterality of, 49–52, 59–60, 127,
    204–205; from women's perspective,
    204; *see also* Kinship *and* Moiety
Melanesia, 15, 23n, 24, 73, 134n, 139
Men's ground, *see* Taraiu
Menstruation, *see* Blood
Moiety, 22–25, 27, 29–30, 58; association
    of tubuan with, 111, 115–118, 154–155,
    157; membership of matamatam spon-
    sors, 125–126; *see also* Big man, Kin-
    ship, Matrilineality, *and* Patrilaterality
Momboto, 19–25, 28–30, 58–59, 65–66,
    74, 172, 174–175, 192, 200–201, 243
Mortuary ceremony, *see* Matamatam

Order, concept of, 15, 19–31, 58–60, 62,
    66, 73, 75, 81, 118–120, 167–168, 170,
    173–174, 200–201, 243–244
Outline of book, 29–31

Patrilaterality, 29–30, 49–52, 148; contrast
    with matrilineality of, 49–52, 59–60,
    127, 204–205; *see also* Kinship *and*
    Moiety
Pollution through sexual contact, 30,
    60–65, 179, 192–193, 196–199
Pospisil, L., 73

Power, 243; absence of concept of personal
    power, 25–26; limits of, 27–29, 66,
    74–75, 81, 123, 174–175; loss of,
    150n, 217; *see also* Big man *and* Di-
    vara

Rabaul, 16, 80n, 129n, 137, 177, 180
Radcliffe-Brown, A. R., 247
Religious divisions, 69, 142
Residence pattern, 40
Ritual, effect of, 19, 32, 243–245, 248, 250
Ritual grades, summary of, 79–81

Salisbury, Richard, 17, 173n, 219
Seclusion of males, 63–65, 101, 192,
    198–199; *see also* Male solidarity
Shell money, *see* Divara
Singing and dancing: by men, 177–178,
    215, 236; by women, 189–190
Social structure: inapplicability of concepts
    of, 23–29, 55–56, 66, 73–74, 92–93,
    122–123, 244, 247–248; loose structure,
    24; traditional anthropological views of,
    24–25, 247
Sorcery, 15, 59, 61n, 112, 174, 182,
    216–218
Symbol, concept of, 248–250

Taraiu, 62, 79, 206–207; first visit to,
    82–88
Taylor, Charles, 19, 245–246
Tolai, 17, 22, 24, 84n, 88–89, 139, 142,
    173n, 177, 219n
Tubuan, 31; association with women of,
    114–115, 118–121; contrast with dukduk
    of, 91–92, 98, 102–104, 107, 110–111,
    151, 154–155, 204–205, 209, 241; con-
    trol by big men of, 224–226, 238; control
    of society by, 123, 167–175, 201, 244;
    learning secrets of, 51–52, 88–90,
    112–114, 117; made by, 145–146, 153,
    155–159; meaning of, 113, 117–118,
    121, 249–250; myth of origin of, 114,
    119; painting eyes of, 166–167; purchase
    of, 110–121

Vunatara, *see* Apik

Women: association with tubuan of, 114–115, 118–121; cooking food during ritual by, 178–179, 181, 207; dependence of society on, 58, 63, 120–121, 200–201; eclipse of ritual activities of, 207; ignorance of male secrets of, 88, 114, 202–204, 217; male attitudes toward, 58–60, 119, 200–201, 242; singing group of, 189–190

KARAVAR

Designed by R. E. Rosenbaum.
Composed by Vail-Ballou Press, Inc.,
in 11 point linofilm Janson, 3 points leaded,
with display lines in Helvetica.
Printed offset by Vail-Ballou Press on
Warren's No. 66 text, 50 pound basis,
with the Cornell University Press watermark.
Bound by Vail-Ballou Press
in Columbia book cloth
and stamped in All Purpose foil.